D1429520

▶ **Remembering Iris Murdoch**

DOI: 10.1057/9781137347909

DOI: 10.1057/9781137347909

palgrave▶pivot

Remembering Iris Murdoch: Letters and Interviews

Jeffrey Meyers

DOI: 10.1057/9781137347909

REMEMBERING IRIS MURDOCH

First published in 2013 by
PALGRAVE MACMILLAN®
in the United States—a division of St. Martin's Press LLC,
175 Fifth Avenue, New York, NY 10010.

Where this book is distributed in the UK, Europe and the rest of the world,
this is by Palgrave Macmillan, a division of Macmillan Publishers Limited,
registered in England, company number 785998, of Houndmills,
Basingstoke, Hampshire RG21 6XS.

Palgrave Macmillan is the global academic imprint of the above companies
and has companies and representatives throughout the world.

Palgrave® and Macmillan® are registered trademarks in the United States,
the United Kingdom, Europe and other countries.

ISBN: 978–1–137–34792–3 EPUB
ISBN: 978–1–137–34790–9 PDF
ISBN: 978–1–137–35241–5 Hardback

Library of Congress Cataloging-in-Publication Data is available from
the Library of Congress.

A catalogue record of the book is available from the British Library.

First edition: 2013

www.palgrave.com/pivot

DOI: 10.1057/9781137347909

Contents

DOI: 10.1057/9781137347909

More than kisses, letters mingle Soules;
For thus friends absent speake.

John Donne, "To Sir Henry Wotton"

DOI: 10.1057/9781137347909

1

Remembering Iris

Abstract: *"Remembering Iris" sketches Iris Murdoch's achievements, her life and loves, and long marriage to John Bayley. The author describes his meetings and interviews with Murdoch; her appearance, environment, skillful teaching, warm personality; her many intellectual interests and tastes; her moral values.*

Meyers, Jeffrey. *Remembering Iris Murdoch: Letters and Interviews*. New York: Palgrave Macmillan, 2013. DOI: 10.1057/9781137347909.

I

Iris Murdoch is now firmly established as one of the greatest English novelists in the second half of the twentieth century. Between 1953 and 1995 she published twenty-six novels, six plays (three originals and three adaptations from her fiction), five books of philosophy, an opera libretto and a book of poetry. Her novels explore erotic mysteries, the quest for personal salvation, and the dark struggles between good and evil. They provide, as Malcolm Bradbury observed, "sensuous pleasures, fantastic invention, high intelligence and moral dignity."[1]

Iris received many honors. She won the £10,000 Booker Prize for *The Sea, The Sea* (when her friend, the philosopher Freddie Ayer, was chairman of the committee), the James Tait Black Memorial Prize for *The Black Prince* and the Whitbread Literary Award for *The Sacred and Profane Love Machine*. She was an honorary member of the American Academy of Arts and Letters, and was awarded honorary degrees from Oxford, Cambridge, Trinity College, Dublin, and Queen's University, Belfast. In 1976 she was named Companion of the British Empire and in 1987 Dame of the British Empire, the equivalent of a knighthood.

Iris' formidable books, still in print, have sold extremely well both in English and in twenty-one foreign languages, and she left an impressive estate of £1,803,491. More than thirty books have already been written about her, including memoirs by A. N. Wilson and by John Bayley (which inspired the film *Iris*), and a biography by Peter Conradi. Her manuscripts are at the University of Iowa; and her library, with many annotated books, her own first editions, some of her letters and Conradi's research papers are at the Centre for Iris Murdoch Studies at Kingston University in Surrey. I believe the ninety-six letters from Iris in this volume (fifteen brief or repetitive ones have been omitted) and three from John Bayley, along with this memoir and our two interviews, will deepen our understanding of her bohemian life and complex work.

After Iris' death in 1999, I read the memoirs and biography to learn more about her life before I knew her. Jean Iris Murdoch, the only child of a father who was a civil servant and a mother who aspired to be an opera singer, was born in Dublin on July 15, 1919. Her Protestant family moved to England in 1920, a year before Ireland became independent. She grew up in London but spent her two-week childhood holidays with the rest of her family in Ireland. She was educated at the high-minded,

DOI: 10.1057/9781137347909

progressive Badminton School in Bristol, where she was a classmate and friend of Indira Gandhi. She then studied classics, ancient history and philosophy at Somerville College, Oxford, from 1938 until 1942, receiving a first-class degree.

As an undergraduate she flirted with Communism and joined the Party to express her solidarity with sufferers. Even someone as morally sensitive as Iris could, by adhering to the Party line (which could suddenly change, as George Orwell observed, while you went to the bathroom during a meeting), remain blind to the political horrors of the Soviet regime: the Ukraine famine, the Purge Trials, the Nazi-Soviet Pact and the Russian invasion of Finland. Cold baths and irregular Greek verbs prepared her to become a junior civil servant at the wartime Treasury, the most prestigious branch of the civil service, from 1942 to 1944. Once there, still full of misguided idealism, she passed information about her work to the Communists.

From 1944 to 1946 she did refugee work with the United Nations Relief and Rehabilitation Administration in Belgium and Austria, and witnessed massive human suffering during and after the war. Many of the refugees were forcibly repatriated to face certain death in Russia, and some of them were machine-gunned as soon as they walked down the gangplank to their homeland. In Brussels she met Jean-Paul Sartre, the subject of her first book, and reading his *Being and Nothingness* brought her back to the study of philosophy at Newnham College, Cambridge, in 1947–1948. She came within the aura of Ludwig Wittgenstein, but was not his pupil. From 1948 to 1963 she taught philosophy at St. Anne's College, Oxford. In 1956 she married John Bayley, an eminent literary critic who would become Warton Professor of English at Oxford, and lived at Cedar Lodge, in Steeple Aston, a village fifteen miles north of the university. From 1963 to 1967 she taught philosophy at the bohemian Royal College of Art in London.

The photograph of the young Iris in the National Portrait Gallery in London reveals an astonishingly beautiful face that, according to the theory of her beloved Plato, reflected the inward beauty of her soul. She had a helmet of blond hair, sparkling blue eyes, square nose, high cheekbones, sensual lips and full breasts. Many sex-starved Oxford students fell madly in love with her and she turned down many proposals.

The influential headmistress at Badminton shared a bedroom off Iris' dormitory with another woman, but she was also a "moral guide" who discouraged intimate friendships among her girls. Her personal example

DOI: 10.1057/9781137347909

gave an imprimatur to Iris' lifelong propensity to lesbian affairs with various butch types, including her best friend, the philosopher Philippa Foot, and an unnamed temptress who once threatened her marriage. She was asked to leave St. Anne's to avoid a lesbian scandal, and lesbianism helps explain Iris' sympathetic portrayal of homosexuals.

Throughout her life Iris was surprisingly, often enchantingly promiscuous—sexually benevolent and generous. As a girl at Oxford she cried when a young man tried to undress her, but later solemnly announced, "I have parted company with my virginity [and feel] relieved from something which was obsessing me."[2] Once she got the hang of it, she became terribly keen on sex—both with those she was attracted to and those she wanted to console. If a man desperately wanted her, he could very often have her. Riveted by "the metaphysics of the first kiss," she wrote that there had never been an impulsive moment "when I have trembled on the brink of such a [passionate] exchange & drawn back."[3] One of her fundamental assumptions was that she had the power to seduce anyone. Alluding to *Crime and Punishment* after she'd been thrown out of lodgings by several indignant landladies, she exclaimed that if they were in Russia, the last one to chuck her out would have been "destined to be killed with a hatchet."[4]

The "shaggy little Shetland pony" could, like Daisy Buchanan in *The Great Gatsby*, smash up things and creatures and then retreat into her vast carelessness. But she too was rejected, first by an Oxford contemporary and then by an emotionally bullying Hungarian. She wept easily and was once seen crying in a bus. When a colleague tried to comfort her, she nervously reassured him with, "I'm quite all right. It's just this love business."[5] In her novels she is not merely an omniscient narrator, but firmly in control of her unruly characters. It's fascinating, knowing about her sex life, to imagine her in the grip of passion or falling short of her own high moral standards. And it's surprising, with all her reckless sexual adventures, that she never got pregnant. There's no evidence that she ever had an abortion (which might have prevented her from having children), though she helped other women procure an operation that was illegal until 1967.

The most notable of her legion of lovers were the English soldier Frank Thompson, the Italian historian of the Roman Empire Arnaldo Momigliano, the Czech anthropologist Franz Steiner and the Bulgarian novelist Elias Canetti. The handsome and heroic Thompson (born in 1920) was tall, thin, fair-haired and brilliant, a gifted poet and passionate

DOI: 10.1057/9781137347909

idealist dedicated to opposing fascism. After parachuting into pro-Nazi Bulgaria and fighting on the side of the partisans, he was betrayed and captured. He nobly affirmed his Communism and (contrary to the Geneva Convention) was summarily executed in June 1944. Thompson and his men all died while raising the salute of freedom. The villagers, Conradi writes, "were sobbing, many present declared the scene was one of the most moving in all Bulgarian history, that the men's amazing courage was the work of an English Officer who carried their spirits, as well as his own."[6] Iris admired T. E. Lawrence, one of Thompson's great heroes and models. Both men were blond, blue-eyed, Oxford-educated Englishmen who led foreigners in guerrilla warfare behind enemy lines. Lawrence carried the plays of Aristophanes into battle; Thompson carried the poems of Catullus. Lawrence had also been captured, but after being tortured and raped had managed to escape.

Momigliano (1908–1987), Steiner (1909–1952) and Canetti (1905–1994)—like her adored Oxford Classics professor Eduard Fraenkel (who lusted for Iris, was allowed to stroke her arm but never bedded her)—were much older, eminent, exiled and physically unattractive European Jews. Their friendship allowed her to continue her refugee work, and satisfied her intense need for father-figures and intellectual gurus. Iris, who felt that "any worthwhile person ought to have at least *some* Jewish blood," declared: "I am practically a Jew myself."[7] The short, bespectacled Steiner, with his scrawny physique and weak heart, was the absolute antithesis of the young, handsome and heroic Frank Thompson. Canetti (no pin-up himself) condescendingly described Steiner as "small and so slight.... His face was uncommonly ugly: a high, receding brow, helpless eyes in perpetual agitation. Weepy speech.... A less attractive person one could scarcely imagine"—all of which profoundly appealed to Iris.[8]

Steiner (the only one of these gurus who was not married) was—like his namesake, countryman and hero Franz Kafka—sweet, frail and sickly, suffering, neurotic and blocked. He too needed an axe to break the frozen sea inside him. His cardiac condition made their lovemaking a precarious and near-fatal event. "In the end it happened," he wrote of his passive role. "But she was afraid because of my heart. Neither of us made a single spontaneous movement."[9] Two weeks later, he described a pathetic and humiliating but deeply moving scene, worthy of the tortured relations of Kafka and Milena Jesenská: "We undressed, but on the draughty sofa my pains became once again severe. She was the more sensible of the two of us, told me to have a rest, and then helped

DOI: 10.1057/9781137347909

me into my clothes. All that with so much concern, goodness, love and tact that this evening brought us closer to each other than a successful union."[10] Soon afterward, Steiner died at the age of forty-three and joined Thompson in Iris' private pantheon of martyrs.

The deaths of Thompson and Steiner left the field clear for the jealous, brutal and monstrous Canetti. In a perverse twist, he came from Bulgaria where Thompson had been executed. John Bayley described Canetti as "squat, almost dwarfish, with a massive head and thick black hair, he looked like a giant cut short at the waist."[11] Like Iris' philosophical hero Ludwig Wittgenstein, Canetti was both brilliantly numinous and destructively demonic. He not only disbelieved in God but also hated Him, and declared "the Day of Judgement would happen when the human race arose with one voice to condemn God."[12] His most influential book, *Crowds and Power*, reduced history to blood-lust, slaughter and a Nietzschean will to power. If the gentle Steiner appealed to her maternal side, the egomaniacal Canetti satisfied her need to submit to a domineering tyrant. Iris recalled that Canettti had electrified her with his sado-masochism: "Physically, he is violent, never quiet, with me. He takes me quickly, suddenly, in one movement as it were.... He holds me savagely between his knees and grasps my hair and forces my head back. His power. He subjugates me completely."[13]

Canetti had several mistresses as well as a one-armed wife who waited patiently in the adjoining room when he took Iris to bed. His malicious description of their first sexual encounter contradicts everything that's ever been written about Iris. Blaming her for his own inept performance, he remarked: "Quickly, very quickly, Iris undressed, without me laying a finger on her.... She lay unmoving and unchanged, I barely felt myself enter her, I didn't sense that she felt anything, perhaps I might have felt something if she had resisted in some form. But that was as much out of the question as any pleasure."[14] Canetti, unlike the gentle Steiner, expected her to play an active role and to arouse *him*. He was, strangely enough, not excited when the beautiful young woman suddenly undressed and was ready for sex. After she left him, he retaliated in a posthumous book. It's difficult to understand Iris' slavish submission to Canetti. But she was intellectually, emotionally and sexually curious, and seemed to have a Lawrencean desire for the extremes of sexual experience.

In 1956 Iris published her second novel, *Flight from the Enchanter* (in which Canetti appears as the evil Mischa Fox), and after three tormenting years finally broke with him. Iris had by then fallen in love with the

DOI: 10.1057/9781137347909

equally bookish and brilliant, yet quixotic and tolerant John Bayley, whose bold attempt to rescue her from Canetti was like Orpheus' trip to the Underworld. Born in Lahore, India (where Kipling's *Kim* begins) in 1925, he was six years younger than Iris. Educated at Eton, he served in the army from 1943 to 1947, and in 1950 earned a first-class degree (as Iris had done) in English at New College, Oxford. John taught at New College and at St Catherine's from 1955 to 1992.

When they desperately needed a place to embrace and kiss, Iris and John instinctively headed for the library. Climbing the iron stairs to an empty stack, they hid among the shelves and held on to each other in the half darkness. John wept with joy. She admired his intellect and moral character, and seduced the timid virgin. After their marriage, they lived in contented squalor—at one point their roof leaked on the exact spot where they lay in bed—for the next forty-three years. But her bisexual love affairs, though less frequent, continued. The English novelist A.N. Wilson, their friend and once Iris' anointed biographer, believed John acted as Prospero, "a sort of controller of the demons and spirits who flew in and out of her consciousness."[15] John gave up writing novels when he married her, and became her stimulating companion and inseparable consort.

There are various explanations of why Iris and John never had children. Her mother got married when she became pregnant, had a difficult birth and didn't want to go through that again. Though amazed that she'd produced such a bright daughter, she perversely hoped that Iris wouldn't have any children of her own. Iris, who had strong maternal feelings, thought children might well have deepened her understanding of human emotions and enhanced her creative life. Was it a conscious decision, as John maintained, or did they leave it in the hands of fate, as Iris said? Speaking for Iris, John told Ian Hamilton that "Iris never in the least wanted children. We've never regretted that."[16] Iris suggested she might well have had children and told another interviewer that it was "my fate, my destiny. There was no particular reason. We left it to the gods, and that's just how things worked out. I never went into the matter."[17] When asked if she regretted not having children, Iris responded, "Not really. I was pretty advanced in years [age 37] from the point of view of childbearing when I married John. Someone [Frank Thompson] I might have married was killed in the war."[18] (Most major women writers, even those who married, did not have children: Jane Austen, the Brontës, George Eliot, Emily Dickinson, Christina Rossetti,

DOI: 10.1057/9781137347909

Edith Wharton, Gertrude Stein, Virginia Woolf, Edith Sitwell, Marianne Moore, Katherine Mansfield, Elizabeth Bowen, Stevie Smith, Olivia Manning, Elizabeth Bishop, Barbara Pym, Carson McCullers, Flannery O'Connor and many others.) It was a great pity that Iris and John never passed their tremendous brain power on to the next generation.

I met Iris in 1978, and over the next seventeen years we continued to meet in England, where I interviewed her for the *Paris Review* "Writers at Work" series. Our correspondence continued until 1995, when she began to be overcome by Alzheimer's disease and could no longer write letters. During that time she published many novels and books of philosophy: *The Sea, The Sea, Nuns and Soldiers, The Philosopher's Pupil, The Good Apprentice, Acastos: Two Platonic Dialogues, The Book and the Brotherhood, The Message to the Planet, Metaphysics as a Guide to Morals, The Green Knight* and *Jackson's Dilemma* (1995).

To put these letters in their proper perspective, it might be useful to say something of myself during the years I knew Iris and John. I taught at the University of Colorado from 1975 to 1992, won a Guggenheim Fellowship for an academic year in London in 1978–1979 and was elected Fellow of the Royal Society of Literature in 1983. I taught for a year each at the University of Kent in Canterbury, the University of Massachusetts in Amherst and the University of Alabama in Birmingham. During these seventeen years, I published nine biographies, wrote four books of literary criticism and edited eight collections of original essays.

I was extremely unhappy at Colorado, but I could not publish my way to a better position. I escaped to Europe every summer and to Mexico or Berkeley—where my brother lived and I had many friends—during the Christmas holidays. In June 1992, after teaching for thirty years at UCLA, Tufts and Colorado, I left academic life, became a professional writer and traded my large house in Boulder for a home in the Berkeley hills.

II

I had always admired the qualities that made Iris Murdoch a great novelist: her technical skill, richness of imagination, philosophical ideas and moral vision. Reviewing *A Fairly Honourable Defeat* in the *Boston Globe* on February 15, 1970, I praised her "compassionate intelligence that asserts the possibilities, however frail, of human love." When I sent her the review, she wrote encouragingly that my interpretation of the novel was

DOI: 10.1057/9781137347909

"on the right lines." She suggested we meet when I next came to England, but I did not feel I knew her well enough to follow up the invitation.

In March 1978 I had a second chance. Iris and John were invited to teach at the University of Denver. They each gave a public lecture—Iris on "Art is the Imitation of Nature," John on "Hardy's Poetry"—and jointly led a two-week seminar on "Truth and Falsehood in Fiction." When my wife and I drove in to attend the seminar from the University of Colorado, we were surprised to find only three other participants. The locals seemed too intimidated to attend a class taught by what journalists had called "the most intelligent couple in the world."

The dimly-lit seminar room gave me my first glimpse of Iris and John. Though bulky now, at fifty-nine, she was still attractive. She had a charming expression, serene yet alert and curious, with short hair, bright, clear-seeing eyes and (as I later discovered when I kissed her cheek) soft, rosy skin. Her face was almost unlined and she used no makeup. But her hair was roughly cut by John and her dress was donnish and distinctly unfashionable: full skirts and shapeless smocks, dark stockings and sensible shoes. She'd worn a shabby raincoat to her wedding ceremony and an old pair of sneakers to her audience with Queen Elizabeth. Like the title of one of her novels, Iris seemed both nice and good. She had, as she said of her father in our *Denver Quarterly* interview, "exceptional integrity, truthfulness and compassion."

Like Professor Calculus in the Tintin books, John was short and bald, with little wings of gray hair sprouting from his skull. He habitually wore a flat cap, food-stained sweater and shabby raincoat, enhanced by dangling shoelaces and mismatched socks, hairy tie and flies at half-mast. He had owlish spectacles, pug nose, deep grooves that ran down from his mouth to his jaw, bulging frog's throat and sweet quizzical expression. Delightfully eccentric, soft-spoken and benign, he managed to steer his dazzling talk through an alarming stutter and hid a formidable intellect behind his self-effacing personality. There was nothing in John's slovenly appearance, hesitant demeanor and apparently clueless character to suggest he'd gone to the posh and snobbish Eton, been an officer in the elite Grenadier Guards and had an older brother who was a brigadier general.

Their seminar focused on the form of the novel, especially in Tolstoy, Dostoyevsky and Mauriac's *Thérèse Desqueyroux*, a novel I'd luckily just read. But their talk ranged freely over all sorts of novels and they responded easily to any topic the students raised. The intimate class allowed me to observe their brilliant, provocative, even mesmerizing

DOI: 10.1057/9781137347909

teaching, both when engaged with each other in an intellectual duet and when they questioned and stimulated us. My mind raced to keep up with them. John had also published novels and they saw literature as creators as well as critics. As in the best kind of tutorial, they brought the students up to the level of the teacher by sharing their ideas and creating a collaborative atmosphere. Humane and highly civilized, both combined penetrating yet entertaining knowledge of the structure, characters and ideas of the novels with lively, down-to-earth and humanly engaging analysis of the meaning. Ever-present in the discussion was the deeper structure of the novels, the presence of the author's mind and spirit. In contrast to the structuralist critics that have largely replaced this type of moral teaching, they recreated and enhanced the experience of reading and invited us to share their responses.

The Rocky Mountain spring was capricious as ever, and slush and ice had lined the streets. As guests of the university Iris and John had been cloistered in Denver, and were eager to break out of Brown's hotel and see a bit more of Colorado. They agreed to spend some time with us in Boulder, and April 4th turned out to be an exceptionally warm and bright spring day. I took them on a campus tour. In our woolen jackets and scarves, we gazed down at the hedonistic students, bronzed already and sunning themselves in bathing suits on the patio of the pool. I pointed out some of the stranger sights of the university: the office of the Gay-Lesbian Caucus (then a rarity on a college campus), the robotic lap-swimmers in the Olympic-sized pool, the grunting brutes in the weight-lifting room, the surrealistic year-round ice rink, the Alferd Packer Grill, ghoulishly named for a convicted cannibal. He was snowed in one winter on a mountain pass and forced to survive by eating his companions. At lunch I introduced Iris to something she'd never eaten—a bagel.

Warm-hearted and sympathetic, Iris was ready to discuss any subject, and had the novelist's curiosity about new people and places. At a small party we held she made sure to talk to everyone, tried to draw each person out and listened attentively to what they had to say. That day our talk ranged over a number of topics, and we discussed both her novels and her life. Among contemporary writers she admired Graham Greene, Saul Bellow and Philip Larkin. But she reread nineteenth-century classics more than she read modern novels. When I asked her why she had so many homosexual characters in her novels, she said she knew so many of them at Oxford. She did not use foreign settings because she had not lived abroad long enough to feel she'd thoroughly understood an alien

DOI: 10.1057/9781137347909

locale. Her only extended residence in a foreign country was when she had worked with refugees in Belgium and Austria after the war. I asked about her attitude to reviews, and she said they weren't sent to her and she rarely read them. She felt that they were usually hasty and superficial, that reviewers and critics often failed to understand what her books were really about. She liked her longtime publisher, Chatto & Windus, and spoke well of the editor, novelist and poet D. J. Enright. She had no agent for her novels; felt her dramatic agent was poor and wanted to get another one. Her earnings were surprisingly small. She had received a modest advance of $2,000 from Viking for her latest novel, *Henry and Cato* (1976), and earned only $600 in American royalties in 1977.

We also talked about Boulder and college life in general. Despite her own sexual freedom, she now disapproved of the current sexual morality of students and felt it would be better if there were less promiscuity. She thought the availability of abortions made men more careless and placed more responsibility for pregnancy on women. When I mentioned that Boulder was the center of American Buddhism and a Tibetan lama taught at the local Naropa Institute, she knew that "Rinpoche" meant "precious one." She was "nearly a Buddhist" herself, would follow the lama if she lived near him and concluded that Buddhism was "the best of all religions."

Iris was perceptive and responsive, calm and self-possessed. She had a great deal of love to give and was loving to the world in general. She was determined to see only the nice and ignore the nasty side of everyone she met. In any case, she would never speak ill of anyone. She either liked most people or, at the very least, was unwilling to criticize them. The warmth of her feelings, her peacefulness and kindness, modesty and generosity, compassion and wisdom shone through her conversation and her letters. But I would have relished her satiric comments on the follies of friends.

III

Iris was such a delightful companion that it was always a pleasure to be with her. She and I had what Goethe called an Elective Affinity: we liked each other and got on well. Our relations were at once like mother and son, respected teacher and favorite pupil, older and younger colleague, but we were also buddies, confidantes and friends. Though we had very different backgrounds and characters—that was part of the

DOI: 10.1057/9781137347909

attraction—we also had some important things in common. We shared some mutual friends: Francis King, Malcolm Bradbury, Alex De Jonge and the Canadian painter Alex Colville. We were both compulsive travelers who knew Italian and had spent a lot of time in Italy, and found that time off for journeys stimulated our work. We were both fond of Berkeley, and her visit there in 1984 had been her happiest experience in America. We strongly disliked the meddling interference of editors and wanted our work to be published as we wrote it. We fought against the lowering of academic standards by the introduction of ideologically driven courses. Iris had opposed the analytical philosophy that flourished in Oxford after the war; I opposed the debasement of literature by the trendy, half-digested literary theory that dominated American academic life.

We both worked hard and published a book every year, and Iris always read and responded to my writing. She felt her role was not to criticize, but to approve. Unlike the colleagues who envied my stream of books, Iris liked and encouraged it. I admired and respected her, and was delighted—even astonished—when she both praised my work and warned me not to work too hard. Since she did not practice dissimulation and had no reason to flatter me, I could only assume that her praise was sincere. As we exchanged books, I read hers with great interest and pleasure, and she seemed eager for my considered opinion of her work. Iris was sometimes worried that I might be "cross" with her and, toward the end of our correspondence and after more than a hundred letters, actually thanked me for writing to her. I eagerly absorbed all she had to say and felt about Iris as she felt about her teacher Eduard Fraenkel: "When I am with him knowledge and ideas seem to flow from him and into me quite automatically."[19]

When corresponding with Iris I tried to write letters that would interest her and to send comments about her behavior and private life I found in the press that would stimulate a lively response. Otherwise, when pressed for time or about to leave on one of her frequent trips, she would simply dash off a quick note. I never got her to explain, for example, the importance of Herbert Spencer and the meaning of Wittgenstein's gnomic pronouncement, "The world is everything that is the case." She always signed off with "love," "much love" or "lots of love." Even if she wrote this way to a lot of other people, I was still pleased to have this precious bit of her affection.

I questioned her about the authors I was studying and described the conferences I attended on Lawrence, Hemingway and the Spanish Civil

DOI: 10.1057/9781137347909

War. I mentioned my travels and work, noted the distinguished visitors and ludicrous events in Colorado, asked about her novels, told her about mutual friends, and discussed the literary gossip in America and England. I regret, in the days before e-mail, that I didn't make carbon copies of my letters to her. Toward the end of her life she burned all the letters she'd received.

Many readers and strangers wrote to ask Iris for advice and assistance. She scrupulously answered most of them and wrote scores of letters to many different correspondents. She spelled words correctly, used many exclamation marks and expressed herself precisely. Iris was always keen for new experiences. Her letters discuss her philosophy and novels, extensive travels, literary friends, past and present writers, paintings, politics, love of Berkeley, A.N. Wilson's never completed biography and delight in swimming, as well as her eagerness to meet on our next trip to Oxford and London and a lively interest in my daughter's education (she hoped Rachel would go to Oxford after graduating from Swarthmore). She decorated one particularly jolly letter with a wavy aquamarine border and five red stars, and apologized for those that were handwritten at a rapid pace and often quite difficult to decipher. Reading them was rather like breaking a code, and as the meaning gradually emerged the contents seemed even more interesting.

Iris did not read much contemporary fiction, apart from books by friends like Antonia Byatt and Josephine Hart, but often discussed the writers she most admired: Lady Murasaki, Dostoyevsky, Tolstoy, Zola, Proust and John Cowper Powys—a great favorite and strong influence on her work. She admired Joyce's story "The Dead" but it's surprising, considering her Irish background and fondness for Dublin, that she didn't include *Ulysses* among her favorites. She may have been put off by its coarseness and low humor, and its satiric portrayal of the Irish.

Though Iris was not known for her humor, she could be quite amusing in her letters. She used phrases like "touchy grandee" and make "an olive branch, or oil on water, move"; described one of my letters flying out of her window during a violent storm; remarked, after a weak chair had collapsed under me at a dinner party, "I'm sure you must be welcome at many other places"; observed that editing collections of original essays involved "stirring up the slow and getting politely rid of the bad"; and exclaimed of the men at Oxford in her time: "the creatures were all over the place."

We also discussed politics in England, America, Gibraltar, Israel and Ireland, where she condemned the evil of the IRA. Though brilliant and

DOI: 10.1057/9781137347909

incisive, Iris could also be muddled, wanting to touch all the contradictory intellectual bases: Communist and Tory, Anglo-Catholic and Buddhist. Like many rationalists—Aldous Huxley and Arthur Koestler are notable examples—she sometimes lapsed into fuzzy mysticism and interest in the paranormal. Above all, she valued truth and moral rectitude. The most extraordinary aspect of her letters to me was her eagerness to apologize for what she considered the slightest misdemeanor or infraction.

John's handwritten letters to me had many of Iris' characteristics, a sign of his imitation or their symbiosis. He also wrote "Rd ," "tho'" and "etc" without a period; used ampersands, parentheses and exclamation marks; underlined many words and signed letters "with love." Both quaintly used "lived" for inanimate objects, as in "the painting lives in Czechoslovakia." He too was naïve about money, sometimes apologetic and always generous in his praise. John and I had once been asked to review Leopoldo Alas' long Spanish novel *La Regenta* (1885). I found it too boring to finish and gave it up. When I asked John how he managed to get through it, he replied, "I didn't actually read it. Just wrote the review."

Iris often mentioned the pleasures of swimming in oceans and lakes—her favorite recreation and strong bond with John. While on holiday in Dorset during a heat wave, she'd spent most of her time in the water. She thought landlocked Oxford would be perfect if it could be "removed" and placed on the coast. She loved the tides of the sea and rush of the rivers, which seemed to resemble the flow of words, and symbolic swimming scenes appeared in novels like *Nuns and Soldiers*. Swimming represented cleanness, relaxation, freedom, even spiritual regeneration as she floated therapeutically in the water, or potential danger (she once nearly drowned) as she surged through the crashing waves. She dearly wanted and could easily have afforded her own swimming pool, but lived modestly and would have considered it extravagant and pretentious.

Iris and I shared a professional interest in painting. She'd taught for five years at the Royal College of Art; I'd published *Painting and the Novel* and a life of the artist and writer Wyndham Lewis. Her travels were closely connected to art. She discussed her visits to museums in Madrid, Paris, Cologne, Oslo, Lugano, and northern Italy, as well as in New York, St. Louis and San Diego. And she specifically mentioned her interest in Benardino Luini, Jacopo Bassano, Edvard Munch and Max Beckmann. Thomas Gainsborough played an important part in *The Bell*, Titian in *Henry and Cato* and *The Sea, The Sea*. Titian's *The Flaying of Marsyas*,

DOI: 10.1057/9781137347909

which she called "the greatest painting in the Western canon," appears significantly in *The Black Prince* and *Jackson's Dilemma*.[20]

Iris explained that she planned her novels in great detail—characters, scenes, the overall structure. Only when she had the shape of the book and the people in it very clear in her mind did she begin to write. She said, "I find inventing a novel very difficult. I can write it quite easily once I've invented it.[21] ...I make two complete drafts, and then revise, paying extra attention to every word. I like writing. I enjoy the English language, and constructing sentences. I like telling stories."[22] When she adapted her novels for the stage, the fictional characters who had existed only in her mind or on her page suddenly took human form and spoke her words. Iris adamantly, if unconvincingly, denied that her characters were based on real people (like Mischa Fox on Canetti), as if that indelicate maneuver would reveal the limitations of her creative powers. I once suggested editing a Viking *Portable Murdoch*, sent her a table of contents and asked for her comments. She liked the idea, but Viking didn't go for it. (Her essays were finally collected in a weighty tome, *Existentialists and Mystics*, 1997.) Three months later, wrongly thinking that I was "cross" with her, she wrote an especially long and interesting letter to placate me.

IV

Over the years we met from time to time in London and Oxford (four more times at her house, four times at mine). On the first of these occasions, December 1979, she and John came to lunch with us in Belsize Park, north London. I was teaching at the University of Kent that year but we were living in Professor John Findlay's house, which I'd rented for the Christmas holidays. As usual Iris and John arrived by tube rather than taxi, and I walked round the corner to meet them at the station. When I told her how well I'd worked that day, anticipating an afternoon with her, she wittily chose to misunderstand me. She remarked, "I *do* hope I'm not disturbing you," as if I might suddenly exclaim: "Quite right! I have to finish an important article. I must skip lunch and ask you to leave at once!" She was impressed that I was writing at the vast leather-topped desk and among the learned tomes, many of them in German, of that distinguished Hegelian, who held a chair of philosophy at the University of London. She knew Findlay's work and said he claimed the non-existence as well as the existence of God could be proved.

DOI: 10.1057/9781137347909

She also discoursed that afternoon on modern writers and academics. She had been reading Thomas Mann and greatly admired his major works, despite obvious faults in *The Magic Mountain*: encyclopedic material that was not well integrated into his novels and pedantic dialogues that went on too long. She asked what else she ought to read, confessing she couldn't face the *Joseph* tetralogy, and I suggested *Lotte in Weimar* and *Confessions of Felix Krull*. She questioned me about Mann's life and exile, we discussed Nigel Hamilton's *The Brothers Mann* and spoke of Heinrich Mann's sad eclipse during his years in America.

John Carey, recently made professor of English at Oxford, she described as lively and hard-working (always a virtue with Iris), though somewhat rebarbative and known as Frosty John. She admired Frank Kermode's learning, but thought him a bit dour, like the Scots. When I said he came from the Isle of Man, she added that that was even worse, for their ancestors were all "elves or something." Asked if there was now a literary center in England where writers met to talk, she thought no such place existed. When I described my disappointment at the lack of social and intellectual life at the University of Kent, she was sympathetic to my plight and annoyed with my colleagues for not making more of the faculty exchange. John said it would be the same at Oxford, but Iris disagreed.

She asked about the centers of structuralism in America. I mentioned Yale, Johns Hopkins and Virginia, which published *New Literary History*, and we spoke of the luxurious academic conferences held at the Rockefeller Study Center in Bellagio on Lake Como. She strongly believed (as I did) that structuralism and semiotics were harmful to both literature and literary criticism. She seemed receptive to my suggestion (supported by John) that she use her authority as a novelist and philosopher to write a devastating critique of these theories and publish it in *Critical Inquiry*, a journal she found interesting. She felt there was a big hole in the center of the structuralists' thinking, and that the Marxists did not feel obliged to use the same logical thought and clear language as bourgeois liberals.

She continued to travel extensively and in October 1979 spent a month in China, as a guest of the government, on a cultural exchange. (John had also been invited but couldn't go because he was teaching.) The group began in Peking, swung in a wide arc west and south, and finished up in Canton and Hong Kong. She was free to walk around and talk to students who approached her on the street and to anyone else who spoke English. China was still recovering from the cultural onslaught of the Gang of

DOI: 10.1057/9781137347909

Four. English books were scarce and the food was terrible, though as guests they had the best available. There was very little to buy, but she was pleased to be wearing a soft blue hat she'd found there. Despite the puritanically restrictive social and sexual life, she was most impressed by the standard of living, employment and education in China.

Our next meeting took place in July 1982. My wife, nine-year-old daughter and I went to lunch with Iris and John at the house in Steeple Aston, where they'd lived since their marriage in 1956. We arrived in a heavy rainstorm, making our way through the wildly overgrown—"we care for it ourselves"—front garden. The large house was run down and seemed oppressively damp and uncomfortable: furniture rickety, slipcovers stained, fire grate full of ashes, books and papers heaped on the staircase and floor. The walls had huge patches of green mold. The cold toilet, with its archaic thunderbox, was filled with language books and dictionaries. (In *Who's Who* Iris listed as her recreation "learning languages.") Iris and John did not go in for creature comforts, but lived in a kind of austere chaos. She touchingly said that John knew how to arrange a room to make it look nice, but there were no signs of his decorating skill at Steeple Aston. The car they drove, an old Renault, was as shabby and as much loved as the house. They kept bringing it in for repairs so they could hang on to it, and had to install a metal plate in the front so their feet wouldn't fall through the rusted hole in the floor. She laughed when I compared it to the paddle boats on the pond of the Boston Common.

It turned out to be a large party, and the other guests, an assortment of eccentric intellectuals who mumbled their unfinished sentences, suggested that Iris was paying off her social debts in one gathering. They included Norah Smallwood, Iris' editor at Chatto; Gina, a young news writer at the BBC whose father taught American literature at Hull; Peta Ady, a lady economics don at St. Anne's; Iain McGilchrist, John's pet student, in pale linen suit and mauve socks, just completing a fellowship at All Souls and about to enter medical school at Southampton; David Luke, a German don at Christ Church; and Professor Chung, a greedy Korean, who monopolized Iris. Chung obviously thought he had reached the promised land. He pulled books off the shelves and insisted—despite her embarrassed reluctance—that she sign and give them to him. I thought she could resist his crude rapacity and might resent it if I tried to intervene with a guest in her house. Later on, I felt very angry that I had not stopped him from taking advantage of her kindness.

DOI: 10.1057/9781137347909

Looking like a deranged but convivial chemist, John concocted a potent brew of champagne cocktail—with bitters, Spanish brandy and French cognac—that threatened to explode. When a curious mouse crawled up John's arm, around his neck and down his other arm, he ignored it (or was perhaps unaware of it) and calmly continued his conversation. Iris spent most of her time fending off the Korean and serving the plentiful food. We had cold chicken and tongue, risotto, salad and cheese, baked beans and olives, hard-boiled eggs with curry sauce. She said less than usual, but did mention that she was soon going on her annual visit to Stephen Spender near Arles, in Provence. Though she planned to write there, she would not stay long because of the press of work. I carried the huge typescript of her latest novel, *The Philosopher's Pupil*, to her editor's car and we left at about four o'clock. Leading us through the wet fronds of the front garden, Iris seemed eager to clean up the gigantic mess in the kitchen (she had refused our help) and get back to her desk.

In October 1983—when I was back in Belsize Park, spending a grant year in London and writing a life of Hemingway—Iris came to dinner. The three of us drank three bottles of wine, but the food was abundant and no one got drunk. Though Iris liked a drink before dinner and a bottle of wine (the cheaper the better) with her meal, I never had the pleasure of seeing her intoxicated. We talked about her family background. Her father's people were lowland Scots farmers and he was born in New Zealand. Her mother's family, the Richardsons, were squires, given land in Ireland after Cromwell's victories. Her father had died in 1958. She was devoted to her mother, now in her eighties, who suffered from Parkinson's disease and senile dementia. Iris came to London once a week to care for her mother, as well as for John's, and they rather dreaded Christmas with the two sick old mums. Just that day she had moved her mother out of a mental asylum and into a nursing home. But she feared that her mother, though much better off, would not be happy there or willing to remain.

Iris remarked that though she was one-hundred-percent Irish, she felt nothing but revulsion for Eire and couldn't go there. She disliked its backward education, lack of contraception, violation of women's rights and fomenting of violence through hopeless promises of union. She had been a friend of the novelist Elizabeth Bowen and a guest at Bowen's Court. It was typical of the Irish government, she said, to break its promises and destroy the house as soon as they had bought it from her.

We talked of geniuses she had known or met. She observed that Bertrand Russell pretended to be a sage and moral guide, but actually

DOI: 10.1057/9781137347909

behaved immorally and was "rather a cad." Ludwig Wittgenstein, whom she knew slightly, had a strong, strange accent. But she did not take much notice of it because she was so busy concentrating on his conversation. He was a genius, impatient with small talk. Disturbed by his own homosexuality, he was also a devil who deliberately caused evil. He abandoned old friends, harshly criticized Jewish refugee-philosophers, told promising students to give up philosophy and ruined many careers. She thought Elizabeth Dipple's study of her work (1982) was competent, but Dipple didn't properly understand Wittgenstein and was quite mistaken in arguing that he provided the philosophical basis of her work.

Apart from Wittgenstein, the only other genius Iris had known was Elias Canetti. He was (she weirdly thought) a good man who could have used his intellectual power, had he wished, for evil purposes. She knew and was impressed by John Searle, professor of philosophy at Berkeley, who had advanced J. L. Austin's ideas, but did not agree with his philosophical position. She did not have a television and was interested to hear about *Voices*, a program in which Searle had debated the mind-brain problem with the neurophysiologist Sir John Eccles. She thought she'd like to appear in that highbrow program.

Iris read and reread classic novels, especially Turgenev, Jane Austen, Dickens, Henry James and Thomas Mann. She'd been through their novels so often that she knew entire passages by heart and sometimes felt anxious that she'd "read all the books." She smiled knowingly when I quoted Stéphane Mallarmé's "*La chair est triste, hélas! et j'ai lu tous les livres.*"

Iris worked all day, but not at night. She was also engaged on a long philosophical work, *Metaphysics as a Guide to Morals* (eventually published in 1992), based on her Gifford lectures at Edinburgh, which would take a long time to complete. She rather disingenuously warned that it would be pointless to try to trace the real-life models of her fictional characters. They were all based on herself, "which I suppose is rather boring."

She wrote in longhand, making three complete drafts, the final one clear and typed by a professional. She'd found Carmen Callil too emotional to direct Chatto & Windus, and had no actively involved editor at Chatto. Later on she said she was getting to like Callil, and thought her mixture of Australian and Lebanese blood was a potent combination. She sent in her novels and they published them as written. I amused her by quoting Disraeli's "When I want to read a book, I write one," and by comparing her to Bulwer-Lytton, who sent his novels directly to the printer and allowed the publisher to read them only *after* they were bound. A

DOI: 10.1057/9781137347909

member of the Royal Society of Literature, she'd won the Booker Prize once and thought neither Salman Rushdie nor anyone else should win it twice. Later on, J. M. Coetzee won it twice.

When I contrasted my intellectual isolation at the University of Colorado (where young people came to retire) with the life I led in London, she was surprised. She said she'd always thought of American towns as close to each other, because she simply got on a plane and flew on to the next place. Having spent her life in Oxford and London, it was hard for her to grasp the sense of vastness and remoteness one experiences in the American West.

Like Doris Lessing, Iris had been a Communist in her youth. She knew some Russian, though not nearly as much as John, but it was not much help on her recent trip to Czechoslovakia. She had a close Czech friend and spoke of how dreadful it was for an intellectual to live there. He'd been imprisoned by the Nazis, and was later jailed by the Communists for deviating from the Party line. She remarked that unlike Communists, who are in a dead end, many religious people, after abandoning belief in youth, rediscover it in old age.

She surprised herself in the recent election by voting, for the first time, for the Tories and Margaret Thatcher (who would make her a Dame), and did so because of the extremely dangerous left wing of the Labour Party. She thought the cabinet minister Cecil Parkinson, disgraced in a sexual scandal, "shouldn't have messed about in the first place," but that it was very wrong of Sarah Keays, who'd become pregnant by him, to condemn him in public and ruin his career. Iris thought she would have been much better off accruing sympathy as the injured party than playing a vindictive role, which she would later regret.

In March 1984 we had dinner with Iris and John at their London flat in Cornwall Gardens, off the Gloucester Road. She had phoned to invite us on a Saturday morning. I was reading comfortably in bed, assumed the call was for my daughter and let it ring. After about twelve rings a guest finally got out of bed and picked up the receiver. "I sensed you were at home," Iris told me. "I *willed* you to answer it." Our guest was most impressed by her persistence. On the way to her flat we came across a scene reminiscent of a Murdoch novel: a bedraggled assortment of tarty ladies' underwear, black and red, strewn across the damp pavement, together with a couple of crisp twenty pound notes. Was this an acrimonious ejection or hasty flight from a domineering lover, a quick payoff or generous donation? I scooped up the cash, but didn't mention

DOI: 10.1057/9781137347909

this windfall to Iris, afraid that she'd somehow disapprove and expect me to make some effort to find the owner.

Their guests (now more congenial than at the lunch in Oxford) included an elderly agent, Lady Avebury; a children's book publisher, Sebastian Walker; a young woman, Mary-Kay Wilmers, then on the staff (and now editor) of the *London Review of Books*; Robert and Shirley Lettwin, he teaching at the London School of Economics, she the author of a book on Trollope; and John Simopoulos, a Greek philosophy don at St. Catherine's (John's college). He reminisced, "I used to review for an important journal… but it packed up twenty years ago!" Oxford also had some dead weight.

The stairs up to the flat were steep, the rooms small, the kitchen rudimentary, but we felt grateful for the warm hospitality. The food was weird— and famously so. On their crowded table we had cold mackerel with lovage, chervil and mayonnaise; two kinds of stew in watery gravy: one with frankfurters, one (John's ghastly specialty) with nettles; store-bought cakes; and many bottles of excellent twelve-year-old wines from the cellars of St. Cat's. Six of them were opened and served at the same time, which rather spoiled the effect. But this evening was not about fine dining. Iris and John were real bohemians—friendly, lively and talkative as ever.

Iris wore an odd, attractive outfit: black breeches and stockings, ruffled blouse and velvet jacket. She'd recently gained weight and looked a bit top-heavy. She didn't have much time to talk while entertaining eight guests, but told me she was terribly overworked. She was writing a philosophy book in the mornings and, as a rest from that labor, a novel in the afternoons. They were soon going to Berkeley, where John would give the Beckman lectures. But they were very vague about where and what sort of place it was, and unaware of its spectacular setting across the Bay from San Francisco. They eagerly asked about places to see and I whetted their appetite by describing the houses of Robert Louis Stevenson and Jack London, the Russian River and Napa Valley, Carmel and Monterey, Big Sur and the Hearst Castle at San Simeon.

Recalling their time in California, John wrote to me early 1987: "We loved Berkeley too—there for a month staying in the Women's Faculty Club—my ideal spot. Strawberry Creek & the redwood trees sighing, & the tequilas in the bar at the Men's Faculty Club! Also *asparagus*, which we bought every day & cooked in the diminutive kitchen at the end of our corridor at the W.F.C. I was in there one day when there was an earthquake & the saucepans banged & rattled—I thought it was a truck going past!"

DOI: 10.1057/9781137347909

V

Normally quite reserved about her personal life, Iris usually had interviews at Chatto's office, academic rooms and other public places. But trusting me as a friend, she let me interview her at home and was unusually frank about herself. Her manner, as always, was gentle but firm. Experienced at interviews, Iris gave without coaxing thoughtful, elaborate answers. She spoke extensively about her life and about larger questions: art, philosophy, morality and religion. But she told me very little about her work habits and creative process, and was guarded about the sources and meaning of specific novels.

Though I've done more than five hundred interviews for my biographies with many eminent people, I felt constrained by my friendship with Iris and did not press her on some sensitive questions—like why she'd never had children—as I would have done if I'd known her less well. Most interviews focused on her work. I was more interested, as a friend and a biographer, in her life than her writing. But that was not what the *Paris Review* wanted. I should have concentrated on one of her best novels, like *The Bell* or *The Sea, The Sea*, and questioned her more extensively about her writing. Did her dreams ever inspire or enter into her fiction? Why didn't she describe lesbian or heterosexual encounters? What was her daily work routine? Another interviewer later noted that "she writes all morning and then fixes herself lunch. Early afternoon is devoted to housecleaning (*sic*), laundry, shopping and correspondence. At 3:30 she takes a half-hour nap, then writes until 7."[23]

I wish I'd also asked her about the relation of her wide-ranging travel to her creative process and her use of notebooks, and more about how she began her novels. She usually started (I later learned) with a "nucleus of two or three characters and some kind of general idea of a conflict."[24] She wrote rapidly, took only three to five months to complete the first draft of one of her long novels and refused editorial advice. Iris once exclaimed: "Part of me wants to be Raymond Queneau, another wants to be Thomas Mann," and she never fully integrated the fantastic and realistic elements in her work.[25] Like her much admired masters—Dickens and Dostoyevsky—she was a hard-working and always driven writer, who started to think about her next novel about half an hour after completing her previous one.

Absolutely sure of herself, Iris didn't even show her work to John, a fine critic who might have improved it. She wrote her novels with characteristic

DOI: 10.1057/9781137347909

idiosyncrasies and imperfections, and didn't want them to be "corrected" by anyone else. She didn't eliminate careless writing and tedious repetition, limit her Russian profusion of characters and simplify her improbably convoluted plots. She recognized serious flaws in her work when her American editor, Marshall Best, pointed them out, but lost interest once the book was finished. Her unwillingness to make a final revision (let alone rewrite an entire book, as D. H. Lawrence sometimes did) occasionally prevented her from realizing her full potential as an artist.

On July 27, 1988 I taped our interview at Iris' new house in Hamilton Road, Oxford, and then took her out to lunch at the local Italian restaurant. I transcribed the tapes and she extensively revised and expanded the typescript, deleting and adding whole paragraphs, and including an entire new page of manuscript. She changed the wording for stylistic reasons and cut passages for clarity, but did not eliminate controversial or personal passages. I sent her first revisions to the *Paris Review*. They asked me to ask her to elaborate some of her answers, which she at first refused to do, and I was caught in the crossfire. Then, after I'd completed what I thought was the final text, she changed her mind and agreed, but did not elaborate the particular points I raised. This led to even more additions, revisions, retypings, submissions and delays.

In December I was distressed to hear that the *Paris Review* would publish the interview only if Iris was willing to answer even more questions, in writing and in her own good time. If she was not willing, they probably would not. Iris certainly knew who she was, what she had achieved and how she stood in the literary world. She also had strict ideas about proper behavior and a streak of genuine humility. Reflecting on her previous refusal to cooperate, she added that she was only being jokily ironical and was, in fact, willing to answer their additional questions.

I finally persuaded the magazine to publish the interview without further response from Iris, and wrote to tell her so. Meanwhile, however, as she explained in a charmingly contrite letter, she had unwittingly complicated and confused my delicate negotiations by agreeing to answer more questions *after* I thought we had the final text and were proceeding to publication. I valued my friendship with Iris much more than the fate of our interview, and was surprised that she felt the need to apologize for the confusion and touched by her concern for my feelings.

The editors then proposed adding to my interview other answers that Iris had given after a lecture on an entirely different occasion in New York. The questions were asked by a writer who had written a nasty

DOI: 10.1057/9781137347909

article about her and whom I particularly loathed. This inevitably caused even more friction. I adamantly opposed this, but the editors included the additions against my will. The questioner wanted his name to appear with mine as the author of the piece and I had to fight to delete it. On top of all this, the *Paris Review* cut my interview in half without consulting me. After many tedious and often acrimonious delays, they finally published the interview, two years after it took place, in the summer of 1990. I published their deletions separately in the *Denver Quarterly* in the summer of 1991. I now include all the substantial deletions that were not published in either interview. Though my troubles continued for two years, in the end at least, Iris was pleased with the two interviews and thanked me for them.

In August 1990 we met for lunch at our rented house in Islington. Iris had come to London that morning and had just been swimming. She'd visited the novelist Brigid Brophy (once her lover), who had multiple sclerosis and could no longer write. She'd had a friendly argument with Brophy, who admired *Anna Karenina* but disliked *War and Peace*. When I mentioned we had been to see *Kean*, she said she didn't much like Sartre's plays, not even *No Exit*, and rarely went to the theater now except to see Shakespeare.

Iris and John had moved in April 1986 from Cedar Lodge, the cold, damp, stone country house in Steeple Aston, to a small suburban brick corner house on Hamilton Road in north Oxford. One weekend, without consulting her, John had impulsively bought this house, which proved unsuitable. After three and a half years in Hamilton Road they became disturbed by the noise and, after being burgled, by nearby "vandalizing elements." I wondered how burglars could ever find the loot or how intruders could vandalize a house that had already been vandalized by Iris and John. In the fall of 1989 they moved to a larger house on Charlbury Road in north Oxford, which they thought would be quieter and have more room for their books.

We met for the last time at their new house in July 1992. John was retiring and had been moving in hundreds of books from his office at St. Cat's. There was not enough room for them and they were piled up everywhere. The front garden was overgrown—Iris was no good at employing people, she said, inside or out—but the back garden, which she tended herself, looked orderly. I brought along an article from the *Independent* of July 31st about Cedar Lodge, which had been turned into a bed and breakfast hotel. Iris didn't want to look at the article and seemed pained

DOI: 10.1057/9781137347909

by the idea of strangers invading her old home. Ever on the move, she and John had just returned from a wet holiday in Cornwall, where they had rented a house and cooked for themselves, walked in the rain and read a lot of books. She was soon going to the country to stay with the widow of Reynolds Stone, who'd illustrated her poetry book, *A Year of Birds*, and would then travel to Italy.

A. N. Wilson was working on her biography but hadn't got very far. She didn't know his publisher (which was Century-Hutchinson) and said he was also writing a novel. He had become involved with another woman and his marriage had broken up. In 1991, when she heard that Wilson had finally given up her biography to write one about Christ, she remarked, "my head is duly bowed." Iris was "appalled" at the idea of having her biography written, yet felt it was inevitable and added, "I do rather hope this matter can be postponed until I have left the scene." When Wilson finally abandoned the project, Peter Conradi took up the baton.

Iris' mop of hair was now wispy and gray, her complexion a bit blotchy and hairs sprouted on her upper lip. She wore an untidy smock, tucked her trousers into her socks and walked with a sailor's rolling gait. We lunched in the same mediocre Italian restaurant, which I liked even less than last time (we agreed about most things, but not about food). She ordered a bottle of cheap red wine, put her head down and rapidly devoured a large meal. It was unnerving to see her concentrate on the food rather than the conversation. She seemed much less lively, curious and responsive than usual; more unfocused, distracted and withdrawn. Instead of lingering at the table, as we always did, she seemed to find conversation a burden and was eager to get home. In the car I said she was a precious cargo and asked her to fasten her seat belt. Smiling, she said, "I'll risk it."

VI

In her last letters Iris began to complain of fatigue and of the oppressive demands made upon her. She found it increasingly difficult to keep up with her correspondence and write her novels. I myself found it difficult to finish, or even start, reading her last novel, which she faithfully sent me. Forced rather than fluent, it now seemed—with its convoluted plot, freakish characters and bizarre sexual entanglements—a tedious reprise of her earlier work.

DOI: 10.1057/9781137347909

In November 1993 she wrote that she received about twenty letters a day from lonely people who desperately wanted attention. She could not bear to have a secretary, had trouble answering them but did so out of a sense of duty. That year the always fluent writer began to express uncharacteristic complaints about the failure of her imaginative powers. I was saddened by her struggles, but grateful that she was willing to confide in me.

I loved and respected Iris, felt grateful for her praise and her friendship, and found almost as much pleasure in thinking about her when we were apart as I did in her company when we were together. I remembered that her aged mother had been stricken by Alzheimer's and felt something bad was happening, but I was unfamiliar with the disease and didn't know what was wrong. I was touched by her desperate need to go on writing and by her struggle to retain her creative ability. Her letters to me revealed her own tragic confusion and heartbreaking decline. As early as 1993 she recorded in her journal, "Find difficulty in thinking and writing. Be brave"—and she always was.[26] Aware, while surrounded by the sea-mists of Alzheimer's, that she was losing her mental powers and clarity of mind, she could say with John Donne: " 'Tis all in pieces, all coherence gone." Finally, as she feared, Iris fell off the high wire and plunged into crippling darkness.

On February 5, 1997 the *New York Times* confirmed what I had feared: "Iris Murdoch, the 77-year-old British novelist, is suffering from Alzheimer's disease.... Ending months of speculation in the British literary world about her writer's block, Professor Bayley...said he first suspected something was wrong about two years ago when she failed to turn up for an appointment with friends. 'She had completely forgotten where she was going so decided to come home. It was so startling.'...Six months ago, she likened her so-called writer's block to being in 'a hard dark place' from which she was trying to escape." In a moving letter to me sent toward the end of 1997, John described Iris as deep in Alzheimer's but sweet as ever, though nothing remained of her noble mind. She spent her last Christmas with the holly and the IV. After refusing to eat or drink, she died on February 8, 1999, a few months after the publication of John's loving tribute *Elegy for Iris*. Her brain was preserved for science and she became the noble flagship in the struggle against Alzheimer's. The Oxford Iris Murdoch Appeal was successfully launched in 2002 to advance research and endow a professorship that focused on the disease.

I am most grateful to Ed Victor, agent for the estate of Iris Murdoch, for permission to publish her letters.

DOI: 10.1057/9781137347909

Notes

1   Peter Conradi, *Iris Murdoch: A Life* (NY: Norton, 2001), p. 595.
2   Conradi, p. 155.
3   Conradi, p. 281.
4   Conradi, p. 317.
5   Conradi, p. 163.
6   Conradi, p. 188.
7   Conradi, pp. 308, 437.
8   Elias Canetti, *Party in the Blitz*, trans. Michael Hofmann, afterword by Jeremy Adler (NY: New Directions, 2005), pp. 115, 117.
9   Conradi, p. 330.
10 Conradi, p. 333.
11 John Bayley, *Elegy for Iris* (NY: St. Martin's, 1999), p. 165.
12 Conradi, p. 354.
13 Conradi, p. 357.
14 Canetti, p. 167.
15 Conradi, p. 402.
16 Ian Hamilton, "An Oxford Union," *New Yorker*, February 19, 1999, p. 73.
17 Hamilton, p. 73.
18 James Atlas, "The Abbess of Oxford," *Vanity Fair*, 51 (March 1988), 86.
19 Susan Eilenberg, "With A, then B, then C," *London Review of Books*, 24 (September 5, 2002), 8.
20 See my essay "Iris Murdoch and Titian's *Marsyas*," *New Criterion*, 31 (February 2013), 30–35.
21 Simon Blow, "An Interview with Iris Murdoch," *Spectator*, September 25, 1976, p. 25.
22 Philip Howard, "The Booker Prize Won by Iris Murdoch," *Times* (London), November 23, 1978, p. 21.
23 Ned Geeslin and Fred Hauptfuhrer, "Iris Murdoch Is Britain's Prolific First Lady of Fiction," *People*, 29 (March 14, 1988), 126.
24 Jean-Louis Chevalier, *Rencontres avec Iris Murdoch* (Caen: Centre de Recherches de Littérature et Linguistique des Pays de Langue Anglaise de la Université de Caen, 1978), p. 84.
25 Conradi, p. 519.
26 Conradi, p. 585.

DOI: 10.1057/9781137347909

2
Letters

Abstract: *The letters from Murdoch to Meyers from 1978 to 1995 cover various topics, including classic writers like Joseph Conrad, D. H. Lawrence and John Cowper Powys, and contemporaries like John Updike and Vikram Seth; her unprovoked quarrel with Rebecca West; production of her play* The Black Prince; *political views, especially about Ireland; delight that women could be ordained as priests; paintings she's seen; conferences attended; extensive travels; and difficulty writing at the onset of Alzheimer's disease.*

Meyers, Jeffrey. *Remembering Iris Murdoch: Letters and Interviews.* New York: Palgrave Macmillan, 2013. DOI: 10.1057/9781137347909.

DOI: 10.1057/9781137347909

Cedar Lodge, Steeple Aston, Oxford [late February 1970]

Dear Professor Meyers,

Thank you for your letter & the review.[1] Yes, I think you are on the right lines. I didn't see the *Newsweek* review & I haven't read *Eyeless in Gaza*.[2] Do write to me again when you & your wife are in England, & we might meet in London.

All good wishes,
Iris Murdoch

1   Meyers, review of *A Fairly Honourable Defeat*, *Boston Globe*, February 15, 1970, p. A-17.
2   Paul Zimmerman, *Newsweek*, February 16, 1970, p. 100A; Novel by Aldous Huxley (1936).

Steeple Aston [early September 1978]

Dear Jeffrey,

What good news that you are in London! [in margin:] and for a good long time![1] We'd love to see you. At present I am rather tied to the house because my mother is staying.[2] But we'll hope to see you before too long & will communicate. All best & love to you both—

Iris

1   Eight years had passed since Iris' first letter to me. During the academic years 1978–1980, I first lived in Hampstead and wrote a life of Wyndham Lewis, then taught at the University of Kent in Canterbury, which made it possible to see them in London during the year as well as on my annual summer trips.
2   Iris was very close to her mother Irene (Rene), who lived from 1899 to 1985.

Steeple Aston [February 8, 1979]

Dear Jeffrey,

I am so sorry! I now recall having received your letter, before Christmas, and I conclude that it was the victim of an odd accident whereby John, opening a window late at night, caused a number of letters to fly out and *disappear* in a subsequent *violent storm!*[1] *Many apologies*. And, again, I am sorry, I fear we can't contribute.[2] This is a time question. I haven't enough knowledge really.

DOI: 10.1057/9781137347909

And John has too many jobs at present. But thank you very much for asking us, and *all* best to the book—and au revoir, & with love

Iris

I usually answer letters properly—sorry about the one that vanished!

1   This amusing incident is quite characteristic.
2   I had invited them to contribute to a book of original essays that I edited, *Wyndham Lewis: A Revaluation* (London: Athlone Press, 1980).

Steeple Aston, Oxford Aug 30 [1979]

Dear Jeffrey,

Thank you very much for your *very interesting* Murry-Mansfield piece. What a business!* [in margin:] *so funny too!¹ We look forward to further writings (of yours). We have been in France on that rather good sort of holiday where you stay in a friend's house and get on with your work!² On return to England the summer is over—we have this experience every year! (One goes on *expecting* the summer—then hey presto it's autumn!) I expect with you the swimming season has not yet merged into the skiing season. I remember those *mauve* alder trees in the spring.³ —Au revoir and all very best to you both & do keep in touch. John sends much appreciation & love. All cordial wishes and thanks, with love from Iris. "Only Murry could write a book called *God*"—⁴

Yes—God!

1   Meyers, "Murry's Cult of Mansfield," *Journal of Modern Literature*, 7 (February 1979), 15–38.
2   They often stayed with Stephen Spender near Arles.
3   Iris fondly recalls the Colorado seasons and landscape.
4   A quote from my article, which continues, "and only he could begin the book with a very long chapter about himself."

Steeple Aston Oxford [October 31, 1979]

Dear Jeffrey,

Thank you for your letter, and how good to know of your continued English sojourn. The Greek island adventure sounds good. No, I don't think [there is] any Gide influence on me. I never developed any concept of him. (I know he was a liberating influence for many.)¹ Let us know

DOI: 10.1057/9781137347909

your London Christmas address. I think we won't be travelling before that, but a Christmas meeting would be fine. All very best to you both, and I hope the lectures are going very well—and all best from John. yours, Iris

1   André Gide (1869–1951) boldly endorsed homosexuality in *Corydon* (1924) and, more covertly, in his novels *The Immoralist* (1902) and *The Counterfeiters* (1925).

Steeple Aston Oxford OX5 3SE Oct 1 [1981]

Dear Jeffrey,

Thank you for your very nice letter. I'm so glad you liked N&S [*Nuns and Soldiers*]. That pleases me very much. (And thanks for the errata, I do care about these.) You are clearly working hard, very good, we have to see the various outcomes *and* travelling. It sounds a fascinating itinerary. We had two such exhausting hols in France & Greece, & are glad to be back in bracing cool old England. It's good news that you'll be at Sussex, a good address & near London. We must have meetings. I'm afraid neither John nor I know anything about J. F. Powers, though others here may. Has he a London publisher?[1] He sounds v. interesting. I wonder if, America-wise, you are thinking of moving to the east coast—or into wicked California? We have very happy memories of Colo—somehow everyone exceptionally nice (*and* the scenery). I knew Olivia Manning quite well in her later years—a darling person.[2] Her husband Reggie Smith (also v. amiable) is around, ex-British Council, and vice chancellor of Londonderry University.[3] A strong ego, to coin a phrase. I hope Chris Hill was enjoyed.[4] Do keep in touch—lots of love and from John.

Yours, Iris.

My philosophy stuff goes on and *on*.

1   The American Catholic novelist J. F. Powers (1917–1999) won the National Book Award for *Morte d'Urban* (1962). He was published in London by the Hogarth Press.
2   Olivia Manning (1908–1980), English novelist.
3   In July 1982 I spent a frantic and fascinating day with Reggie Smith, the exact model for Guy Pringle in Manning's *The Balkan Trilogy* (1960–1965) and *The Levant Trilogy* (1977–1980).
4   The British historian Christopher Hill (1912–2003) lectured at Colorado.

DOI: 10.1057/9781137347909

Steeple Aston Oxford Oct 28 [1982]

Dear Jeffrey,

Many thanks indeed for sending offprints and tempting news of forth-coming events! [in margin:] Very interesting—I'm fascinated about VG and WL [Van Gogh and Wyndham Lewis].[1] We salute you. We imagine you gazing out on beautiful red trees, distant snows, and then going for a swim in that magisterial warm pool![2] Here we have, apart from beginning of Michaelmas term, never a favourite time, the usual parade of autumn colour, mist, rain, the coal strike still on etc. Soon (perhaps now) all your students will be out skiing in the sun. We look forward to your return here. Thank you for keeping us in touch. Be well, don't work *too* hard, tho' we know you love to! All best wishes & love

Iris and John

1   Meyers, "Van Gogh and Lewis' *The Revenge for Love*," *Modern Fiction Studies*, 29 (Summer 1983), 234–239.

2   Iris was deeply impressed by the huge pool at the university.

Steeple Aston Oxford [late 1982]

Dear Jeffrey,

So glad to hear from you. Hope all goes happily in the east. I'm sorry about TLS. I think it may indeed just be that they don't send books to USA—they always seem to be rushing round in a hurry at the last moment to send off books for review! I will certainly mention *DHL & Italy* and the *Disease & Novel* book (marvellous subject, no wonder the doctors were fascinated) to Chatto.[1] The latter may of course already have an English publisher. We do hope you will all be coming to England soon, let us know of course. I'm so glad Rachel liked the Hampstead school. I hope you'll enjoy *The Philosopher's Pupil*, with which you already have that important connection![2] You're lucky to have such an interesting book to take you to Key West.[3] We've never been there but understand it to be paradise. (John Williams has a house there.)[4] With love, and to Valerie & Rachel, and from John,

Iris

1   Meyers, *D. H. Lawrence and the Experience of Italy* (Philadelphia: University of Pennsylvania Press, 1982) and *Disease and the Novel, 1890–1960* (London: Macmillan, 1985).

DOI: 10.1057/9781137347909

2 I helped publication by carrying the typescript of this novel from Iris' house to the car of her editor Norah Smallwood.

3 I visited Hemingway's house in Key West in the course of my research for his biography.

4 Probably the American composer (born 1932).

Steeple Aston Oxford OX5 3SE March 17 [1984]

Dear Jeffrey,

We are absolutely thrilled and so grateful and pleased! *Yes,* we wd be very glad indeed and proud to be dedicatees of your Hemingway![1] We shall be delighted to see ourselves in real print inside your book, which we shall be so pleased also to read! (I think we'll be Iris Murdoch and John Bayley.) How very kind of you to think of this, we are very touched indeed. It was a great pleasure to see you & Valerie chez nous. I'm glad you're going to be around here for a little while yet, so we can tell you of our American adventures (I hope they won't be awful). We shall hope to see the places you mention.[2] It all seems very through-the-looking-glass at present, & I'm at the stage of not wanting to go at all. I was cheered up to learn from you that Berkeley is by the sea (bay, anyway)—I thought it was miles inland! Thanks again so *much* for your thought about the book. It's a most cheering & lovely event! Thank you—and best best wishes to you both—and thank you too for the fine bottle of wine—and lots of love from Iris.

[Postscript by John Bayley:] A *very* kind idea! I've enjoyed the Hemingway [article] & a fascinating piece on Wyndham Lewis in fiction.[3] Critically really instructive! J.

1 Meyers, *Hemingway: A Biography* (NY: Harper & Row, 1985).

2 I urged Iris and John to see Lake Tahoe, Yosemite National Park, Santa Cruz and Santa Barbara.

3 Meyers, "Wyndham Lewis: Portraits of an Artist," *London Magazine,* 20 (April–May 1980), 61–76.

Steeple Aston June 15 [1984]

Dear Jeffrey,

Thank you very much for your letter and *please excuse* this late reply. Alas we cannot manage those days. We have been very taken over in the last 4-5 days by the sudden death of our friend, and close neighbour here, the writer Michael Campbell (alias Lord Glenavy—there was a

DOI: 10.1057/9781137347909

pretty scrappy *Times* obituary on Wednesday).[1] About four weeks ago his doctor was still thinking he had a virus infection. The cancer was then discovered, very advanced. We have had to help & look after his friend (Michael was queer (gay)) with whom he'd lived for 20 years, also our friend, who is in a terrible state of shock & misery. Michael wrote one good novel called *Lord Dismiss Us*—& other decent novels and very funny things in the *New Yorker*.[2] He was Anglo-Irish & knew my sort of Irish world, & places of my childhood. The funeral is today.

Tomorrow we are going to stay with David Cecil.[3] And the next week days are unfortunately no good because of a lot of longstanding End of Term fixtures, and my having to go to Leamington Spa to fetch some pictures. We are very sorry. We wd have liked very much to see you and talk a lot before your departure. You have been working very hard! So glad about the Hemingway. (And the conference—that should be fun.)[4] I gave a prize to Timothy Mo [in margin: v. nice boy] for *Sour Sweet* at a Society of Authors prize giving—I mean I handed over the cheque![5] Berkeley was delightful. Wd love to talk of. Bon voyage anyway & come back soon again—with love to you both, and from John

[in a circle:] I

1   Michael Campbell (1924–1984), English novelist.
2   *Lord Dismiss Us* (1967) was about homosexuality at an English Public School.
3   The English biographer Lord David Cecil (1902–1986) had been John's teacher at Oxford.
4   I was going to attend a Hemingway conference in Madrid.
5   *Sour Sweet* (1982) by Timothy Mo (born 1950), a novel about Chinese in London.

Steeple Aston Oxford July 10 [1985]

Dear Jeffrey,

Please excuse this late reply to say thank you for sending your *Beckmann* article, with kind quotation from Henry Marshalson![1] What a great painter—I love him—we saw a lot of his work in St. Louis Art Museum, & saw a good deal of private stuff too, property of one Buster May. (He is dead now alas—I hope he left the paintings to the Art museum.) Just lately we came across 6 wonderful Beckmanns in the museum in Cologne.

Do let us know if you'll be installed in London this summer. (The weather is now warm, even hot, not like June.) I am just this moment

DOI: 10.1057/9781137347909

going to Ireland to visit Trinity Coll, & after that we are going to Scotland, we'll be away at intervals but never for very long.[2] With my very best wishes & love to you both, & from John,

yours Iris

1   Meyers, "Review of Carla Schulz-Hoffmann, ed., *Max Beckmann: Retrospective*," *National Review*, 37 (May 31, 1985), 44–45. Max Beckmann (1884–1950) was a German painter, Henry Marshalson a character in Iris' novel *Henry and Cato* (1976).

2   Iris did not mention that she was awarded an honorary D. Litt. by Trinity College in July 1985.

Steeple Aston Oxford Nov 1st [1985]

Dear Jeffrey,

   We are so thrilled about the Hemingway book and the *dedication*! It is so kind of you—and we feel so proud! It's a very special and moving present, and we are delighted![1] I think it is a marvellous book, full of story and thought. Your energy and concentration, as well as wisdom, are remarkable and your writing delightful as well as learned & deep! We thank you for all that—and look forward to the next ones, which sound so interesting—I shall be especially glad to see the Lowell book.[2] *And* to see you both in London next summer! That'll be great. I hope San Diego was fun and warm! We could do with some continued sunshine here, tho' October has been lovely. All very very best to you, and with so many thanks and with love,

Iris

[added from John:] Dear Jeffrey. What a book it is!—I really am full of admiration & the reviews are too. I could add a bit to my Lawrence *if* there is time—will send you a slightly longer & better version in a few days, unless that is intolerably inconvenient.[3]

1   I assumed Iris and John had received many dedications and was surprised by their enthusiastic reaction to mine.

2   Meyers, *Manic Power: Robert Lowell and His Circle* (London: Macmillan, 1987).

3   John contributed an essay on "Lawrence and the Modern English Novel" to a book of original essays I edited, *The Legacy of D. H. Lawrence* (London: Macmillan, 1987).

DOI: 10.1057/9781137347909

68 Hamilton Rd Oxford OX2 7QA [April 23, 1986]

Jeffrey dear, thanks so much for sending the lovely and interesting piece about you at home—we like it very much.[1] Please note our *new address.* We have left old rambling Cedar Lodge and moved into a small warm house in Oxford—in Summertown, you know, the northern "garden suburb." It has all been a great shock, but very wise, and good too! Will you be over in the summer? I hope there will *be* a summer. There hasn't been a spring yet. With best love and from John,

Iris

1   John Farrell, "At Home with Jeffrey Meyers," *Denver Post: Empire Magazine,* March 9, 1986, p. 40, interview about Hemingway.

68 Hamilton Rd OX2 7QA NB: QA May 17 [1986]

Dear Jeffrey,

What a super letter, thank you very much—your power and energy are so impressive! What a great amount you did, achieved, during your visit![1] And so many books in prospect. Well done. I like the Mother Teresa jest![2]

It's good news that you'll be in England. We may be away part of that time but I think not all. Anyway *be sure* to get in touch. Au revoir and lots of love,

Iris

1   In England, in March 1986, I had a publicity tour, organized by Macmillan. for my *Hemingway.*
2   I said I was the Mother Teresa of biographers, trying to rehabilitate literary lepers like Lewis and Hemingway.

[To Valerie. On stationery decorated by Jacques Le Moyne de Morgues' 16th-century *Hautbois Strawberry* in the British Museum.]

68 Hamilton Rd Oxford OX2 7QA Tel 0865-59483 [fall 1986]

Thank you so much for the beautiful jaguar & the news.[1] How nice to be in Berkeley[2] —(plausibly said by Richard Wollheim to be the most wonderful place in the English-speaking world).[3] We *loved* being

DOI: 10.1057/9781137347909

there—living in the Women's Faculty Club, lulled to sleep at night by Strawberry Creek! I'm glad to hear Rachel likes Berkeley High—which must be a very lively spot for learning things. The Berkeley air is good for thought, and I can imagine you and Jeff are full of projects. We are much enjoying the smallness and warmth of our new house! Very good close shops too. We *loved* the Berkeley shopping & lived on asparagus! Do hope we'll see [you] in the summer. John sends love. Lots of love to you both,

Iris

1 Drawing of a jaguar by the French artist Henri Gaudier-Brzeska (1891–1915).
2 I was a visiting scholar at Berkeley during 1986–1987.
3 Richard Wollheim (1923–2003), an English philosopher who taught at Berkeley. Iris was very fond of this quote and used it four more times. I've deleted the repetitions.

68 Hamilton Road, Oxford [April 6, 1987]

Dear Jeffrey,

Thank you so much for sending us your story! It is moving and elegant and sad and full of atmosphere. You must write a lot more stories—perhaps you have done so already.[1] It is a very difficult form. I wrote *one* short story, because a publisher asked for one for a series; it took me ages and was not a success![2] John has been writing *about* short stories lately.[3] You must write some others, set in all sorts of places. I hope you are enjoying Berkeley, where we once spent a very happy time staying in the Women's Faculty Club—an ideal spot, and very close to the bar. Such a lovely town too, with wonderful lotus-eater super-markets. We have just been (2 weeks) at Tulane university and enjoying New Orleans sights & sounds & food. We hope we'll see you both this year. With love, and from John, Iris.

1 Meyers, "A World Historical Moment," *Arizona Quarterly*, 42 (Winter 1986), 344–350.
2 Murdoch, "Something Special," *Winter's Tales* 3 (London: Macmillan, 1957), pp. 175–204.
3 Bayley, *The Short Story: Henry James to Elizabeth Bowen* (Brighton: Harvester, 1988).

DOI: 10.1057/9781137347909

68 Hamilton Road Oxford April 28 [1987]

Dear Jeffrey,

Thank you for your super letter written on Shakespeare's birthday. What a wonderful cruise you were on, floated onward by Conrad, Malraux, Orwell & Theroux—those very interesting characters![1] [in margin: And thanks for the Jarrell piece.][2] Hong Kong is certainly a shock—though coming from mainland China it can seem like home! I envy you all those ports of call. Yes, I thought I recognised the shadow of G. Brenan in your story.[3] I know a bit about him through Honor Tracy (do you know her? A superbly funny & delightful novelist) she was a friend of his.[4] I wish I'd met him. I hope you are writing MORE stories. I am very impressed by your 14 books prospect—well done—you enjoy it all and communicate your enjoyment.[5] I will remind John of your March 26 invite.[6] I can imagine your loving Berkeley—the little town is so nice, it's all so civilised. We loved it. We enjoyed our short stay at Tulane. But I was erroneously expecting a huge lush Mississippi delta just outside the university. I'm sorry you won't be in England—but how lovely to be in California, up & down the coast.

I am sorry to hear of your brother's illness—I hope he may continue better.

Keep in touch, best wishes to your writings, best love to you & Val. And from John,

yours I.

1   In January 1987 I lectured on these authors on a Pearl cruise to Asia. André Malraux (1901–1976), French novelist, art historian and Minister for Cultural Affairs. Paul Theroux (born 1941), American travel writer and novelist, author of *The Great Railway Bazaar* (1975) and *The Mosquito Coast* (1981).

2   Meyers, "Randall Jarrell: The Paintings in the Poems," *Southern Review*, 20 (Spring 1984), 300–315. Jarrell (1914–1965) was an American poet and critic, author of *Losses* (1948) and *Poetry and the Age* (1953).

3   Gerald Brenan (1894–1987), the greatest English writer on Spain, was a neighbor and friend when I lived in a village near Málaga from 1971 to 1975. The story was about my last visit to him in a London nursing home.

4   Honor Tracy (1913–1989), novelist and travel writer, also wrote about Spain.

5   I'd published fourteen books since coming to Colorado in 1975.

6   I'd asked John to contribute to my collection of original essays *The Biographer's Art* (London: Macmillan, 1989).

DOI: 10.1057/9781137347909

68 Hamilton Rd Oxford June 4 [1987]

Dear Jeffrey,

Thanks so much for your letter. Your industry & ubiquity is so wonderful! Well done. And we understand how you want to stay on in dear old Berkeley, charmingest place. No, I've never met G. Greene—he is hardly ever around in England, so far as I know.¹ Ah, Paris in the 1920s.... I've just been there, always charmed. Thanks for sending the interesting piece by Amin Malak!² He has ingeniously put together those 2 old papers to credit me with a theory of fiction! In fact (of course) I have none—except that I think people shd write well! Also he touchingly imagines too that critics (or "critics") can always practise what they preach! (Parsons can't, philosophers can't.) I haven't seen the *Good Father* film (hardly ever see films) or read the N. Lewis book—but note these.³ I have a novel coming out in September (England) January (USA). My present one is not very far advanced.⁴

No—I've never written about that strange post-war refugee adventure—it was certainly weird & amazing—but somehow I've never wanted to write it down.⁵ Best wishes to *your* writing—& from John—with lots of love, I

1   Graham Greene (1904–1991), English novelist, lived in Antibes, in the south of France.
2   Amin Malak, "Iris Murdoch: Liberalism and the Theory of Fiction," *Arizona Quarterly*, 43 (Spring 1987), 19–28.
3   *The Good Father* (1985), a film with Anthony Hopkins. Norman Lewis (1908–2003) was a British novelist and travel writer whose best book is *Golden Land—Travels in Burma* (1952).
4   *The Book and the Brotherhood* was published in 1987, *The Message to the Planet* in 1989.
5   From 1944 to 1946 Iris did refugee work for the United Nations in Belgium and Austria.

68 Hamilton Road Oxford OX2 7QA June 20 [1987]

Dear Jeffrey,

Thanks so much for your letter (hope you can read this one!). Greetings in your new house with super view of the Bay. We envy you the sun (none here). My new novel (out here Sept, in USA January I think) is called *The Book and the Brotherhood*, and is about many things, including Marxism and

DOI: 10.1057/9781137347909

various attitudes to it among the characters who were all Marxists when they were young (but now not). I'm glad you like Andrew (A. N.) Wilson's novels. He is a former pupil of John's, wanted to be an Anglican priest, but then decided not, used to teach in Oxford, but now is freelance literary man (perhaps still does a little teaching). He's married to a clever girl who is an English don, fellow of Somerville (Katherine Duncan-Jones). They are both very nice. His latest novel (called *Stray*) is written from the point of view of a cat. I've read two or three of his novels with great pleasure—I think he's v. good & getting better. He's charming and clever and altogether delightful.[1]

I'm so glad to hear of your autobiography—such a good idea—will much look forward to reading it. Onward!

Thanks for news of the new Bellow novel.[2] Rotten old Macmillan—I hope you'll go to someone else (for Tolstoy). Just going to Wales for a week (no other holiday plans).

With love & best wishes, & to Val, Iris

1   A. N. Wilson (born 1950) later provoked Iris' disapproval by leaving his wife, Katherine Duncan-Jones. His satiric but perceptive memoir is *Iris Murdoch As I Knew Her* (2003).
2   Saul Bellow's latest novel was *More Die of Heartbreak* (1987).

68 Hamilton Rd Oxford [July 30, 1987]

Dear Jeffrey,

Thanks so much for your letter, excuse this in haste, just going away, to say *of course* John wd be very glad to be a referee, best of luck.[1]

I am most impressed, indeed awed, as always by your industry—don't work *too* hard tho' I know you love it. I'm working as usual on philosophy & novel. A novel is coming out in England in September (I think in January in USA). I have also been to India, France, Italy, and am shortly going to Sweden and then Italy again. Why does[n't] one just *stay* in one's room & think?[2] Thanks for the catalogue piece—if those are all 1st editions it's a bargain.[3] I look forward to reading you, especially on T. E. Lawrence whom I (unlike many here) *love*.[4]

And with love to you, I

1   John recommended me as a University of Colorado Research Lecturer.
2   Iris alluded to Blaise Pascal's *Pensées* (1670): "all human evil comes from this, man's being unable to sit still in a room."

DOI: 10.1057/9781137347909

3   I sent Iris a catalogue from R. A. Gekoski with prices of her books.
4   Meyers, *T. E. Lawrence: Soldier, Writer, Legend* (London: Macmillan, 1989).

68 HR OX2 Sept 11 [1987]

Dear Jeffrey,

Thanks you very much for your letter and welcome home from your adventures! By the way, I seem to have 2 addresses for you—Glenwood Avenue & Glenville Drive—I imagine the former is correct. Sorry to have been laconic about my travels. I met Han Suyin and Vikram Seth in Delhi, and John Updike (lately) in Gothenberg.[1] HS is somehow amazing, so handsome. VS is utterly enchanting, and JU *very* beautiful. I expect you know the 2 latter well, perhaps the former too. I have always felt connected with India & *love* being there (have only been twice). It is all connected with having read *Kim* when I was about 8. (And many times since.) And I was at school (progressive left wing boarding school) in England with Indira Gandhi, with whom I remained friends.[2]

I am shortly going to Italy to see pictures.

I envy you that *rain forest*.[3]

With love & best wishes,

Iris

1   Han Suyin (1917–2012), a Eurasian novelist, best known for *A Many-Splendoured Thing* (1952). Vikram Seth (born 1952), an Indian writer and author of *Two Lives* (2005). Gothenberg is in Sweden.
2   Indira Gandhi (born 1917), four-times prime minister of India, was assassinated by Sikh extremists in 1984.
3   The rain forest was in Olympic National Park in Washington.

68 Hamilton Rd Oxford [September 14, 1987]

P.S. I forgot to answer your important question.

God created the world out of an uncontainable overflow of love. ("*Ebullitio*" is the word used by Eckhart.)[1]

With love, I

1   Meister Eckhart (c.1260–c.1327) was a German theologian, philosopher and mystic. *Ebullitio* comes from the Latin word for boil up, produce in abundance.

DOI: 10.1057/9781137347909

68 Hamilton Rd Oxford [October 7, 1987]

Dear Jeffrey,

Excuse in haste, just going away (tho' not for long) to say yes, I'd be very glad, & feel honoured, to be interviewed by you for *Paris Review*!

I'm glad you've settled in again after travels, conquered the garden, & done so much work, *and* discovered a new restaurant. I hope you are still playing tennis in the sun. No sun here. I've asked Chatto to send you latest novel—

With lots of love, Iris

68 HR OX2 [October 31, 1987]

Dear Jeffrey,

Thanks so much for the long letter! I've passed the relevant matter on to John. I look forward to our August conversation. I (and John) interested about Spanish war in Texas conference. We were *very* impressed by Texas & our Austin visit! (very Texan.) John is pro-Brodsky (compares him with Auden).[1]

I haven't been anywhere very romantic lately—just round about England! May even get to Cambridge. Oh yes, we were in Italy and Switzerland—maybe I didn't report—looking at pictures, especially the Thyssen collection in Lugano, where some paintings from the Hermitage were on show. I love being in Italy—just anywhere, makes one feel carefree!

Au revoir & with love & from John, I

I expect you heard of our "hurricane"—Oxford escaped, but London lost *so many trees*. Very sad.

1   Joseph Brodsky (1940–1996), a Russian-born poet and protégé of the English poet W. H. Auden, won the Nobel Prize in 1987.

68 Hamilton Rd Oxford [November 20, 1987]

Dear Jeffrey,

Thanks you for your letter and news—I'm interested to hear about Donoghue—and about the huge deer![1] I note you may be thinking of moving house—and I hope you will get to Lake Maggiore. Yes, it is indeed true that my publisher (Chatto) paid Michael Holroyd £650,000

DOI: 10.1057/9781137347909

for the Shaw biography![2] This has caused some raised eyebrows. I entirely agree with your view of Shaw.[3] I'm sorry to hear Marxists are in fashion again—just as we seemed to be getting rid of those post-post-structuralist blighters.[4] (A Yale acquaintance writes speaking of "post-Rhetoricism" and "New Historicism").

I'm afraid I haven't read Peter Conradi's book*—I had some discussions with him when he was writing it.[5] I like & respect him very much. He is, incidentally, a Buddhist.[6] (And he can stand on his head.)

With love, Iris
*Can't read books about self.

1   Denis Donoghue (born 1928), Henry James Professor at New York University, lectured at Colorado.
2   Michael Holroyd (born 1935), English biographer of Lytton Strachey, Augustus John and Bernard Shaw (4 volumes, 1988–1992).
3   I thought Shaw was a windbag and his plays were a bore.
4   The only Marxists outside of Albania and North Korea had well-paid academic jobs. The former director of the University of California Press later told me that he regretted publishing books on that subject.
5   Peter Conradi (born 1945) published *The Saint and the Artist: A Study of the Fiction of Iris Murdoch* in 1986 and *Iris Murdoch: A Life* in 2001.
6   Iris had a soft spot for Buddhism.

68 Hamilton Rd Oxford Dec 16 [1987]

Dear Jeffrey,

Thanks so much for your letter. I'm glad you have met someone called Eckhart Schutrumpf. That is an achievement. Your industry continues to impress. *Magic Mountain*, yes.[1] I heard the film of Joyce's *The Dead* (a work I *revere*) reviewed and it seemed as it wasn't too bad.[2] I hope the audience were in tears. There's something very special about Dublin in that story—more than anywhere else I can think of. I note that you are off to Berkeley where you are making another home. I like to picture you touring the restaurants & bookshops. I hope the warm weather lasts (lasted) till you reach (reached) California, over those mountains.

Here (in Oxford) we avoided the amazing hurricane that shook London & South East, & it is still clement, damp, not yet cold. A (new) American young friend, brought up in Louisiana & California & coming to England (& Europe) for the first time at Christmas has *never seen*

DOI: 10.1057/9781137347909

snow. I hope there will be just a little, rather pretty. Very best Christmas & New Year wishes & love to you both,

Iris

1   I often taught and wrote about my favorite novel, Thomas Mann's *The Magic Mountain* (1924).
2   John Huston's last film (1987), based on James Joyce's greatest story (1914), is a masterpiece.

68 Hamilton Road Oxford January 16 [1988]

Dear Jeffrey,

I am surprised and upset to learn that V[ictoria] Glendinning says in her biography that R[ebecca] West believed SPLM [*The Sacred and Profane Love Machine*] was based on her family.[1] You say "is this true?" If you mean did she believe this, *yes*. If you mean *did* I base the book on her family misfortunes, *of course no!*[2] I knew, and indeed know, very little about Rebecca West's private life, and I have not read VG's book—and, needless to say, I do not base my stories upon other people's lives, or portray other people.[3] I *invent* people and stories, and regard with horror the idea of exhibiting the adventures or misfortunes of real people in my fiction. To have done this to Rebecca West would have been a disgraceful & unkind act, of which I trust anyone who knows me would know me to be incapable.[4] [double vertical lines on left margin:] Could you please tell me whether Glendinning's book implies that I *did* base the novel on RW's situation?

I had of course no notion that RW entertained this curious belief, and was puzzled by her coldness, even rudeness to me at one or two parties. I was scarcely even acquainted with her, had never had a conversation with her, and this as it seemed gratuitous attitude surprised me. Then one day I got a letter from her asking whether what she believed was the case, and saying that from what she heard about me & her impression of me she had begun to doubt whether I had done this unkind thing. I wrote back saying of course I was not portraying her family life of which I knew nothing and hoped she would acquit me of any such rotten act. She sent a very warm and friendly reply saying she believed me and was sorry to have entertained such suspicions of me!

DOI: 10.1057/9781137347909

I have written to Chatto's about the defective book.[5] With love & best wishes, Iris. [on envelope:] And thank you for piece on *duels* just come.[6]

1   Victoria Glendinning, *Rebecca West: A Life* (1987). Iris' novel was published in 1974.
2   Defining precisely what she means was an important part of Iris' philosophical training.
3   Rather disingenuous. Like all novelists, Iris based some characters on real people, most especially her Central European lovers, Franz Steiner and the demonic Elias Canetti.
4   Iris' agitation was expressed in this contorted sentence.
5   Chatto & Windus was Iris' longtime English publisher.
6   Meyers, "The Duel in Fiction," *North Dakota Quarterly*, 51 (Fall 1983), 129–150.

68 Hamilton Rd Oxford [February 3, 1988]

Dear Jeffrey,

So sorry to be still confused about your address! Will try to do better! Carmen Callil, head of Chatto's, asked you to send the title page of BB [*The Book and the Brotherhood*] back & you will receive a replacement copy, with apologies.

Please could you let me know about the *implication* of the Rebecca West fantasy? Perhaps cd you Xerox the passage in question? I don't want to have to read the book. A letter to the TLS may be necessary, as what is involved is so horrible (I mean that she believed). I told no one about RW's letter to me, [in margin:] and did not imagine that her false belief would be made public.

I hope all goes well on your front! I am struggling unhappily with my novel!

With love, Iris
Chatto & Windus, 30 Bedford Square, London WC1

68 HR OX2 [February 15, 1988]

Dear Jeffrey,

Thank you for writing. VG's [Victoria Glendinning's] words don't seem to me quite strong enough, but no doubt it's better to let the matter drop. It was [a] perfectly shocking thing to be accused of.

I was amused by your description of the Awful Conference in Texas— tho' I'm sure at the time it was exceedingly tiresome! There are such awful

DOI: 10.1057/9781137347909

conferences, alas. We must become a detached spectator, meditating on human folly. Our next "conference," which I hope will be a pleasanter one, is the PEN one in Cambridge in April. I hope to meet again there that enchanting boy Vikram Seth (author of the great California novel, in verse, in the metre of *Eugene Onegin*.)[1] I met him in Delhi last year and liked him very much, a very talented & charming young fellow. Hope it's not too cold with you. We've had an amazingly warm winter *so far*, spring flowers coming up! With love & best wishes,

Iris

1　Iris was quite taken by Vikram Seth and his book *The Golden Gate* (1986). *Eugene Onegin* (1835), a Russian novel in verse by Alexander Pushkin (1799–1837).

68 HR OX2 Feb 18 [1988]

Dear Jeffrey,

Thanks very much for your letter of Feb 13 sending the Xerox of VG book which makes the matter clear—I'm most grateful to you!

It's [a] sad story about the philistine women & blacks invasion. Oxford now has (against opposition from John etc.) *women's studies*. John even had to set an exam paper in these so called studies—he looked at previous papers which had contemptible questions, requiring knowledge of "women's literature," i.e. latest books published in USA. He composed some good questions which demanded thought & having read some real literature. (Better not mention this, it might get round!)

I've heard of *The Walnut Trees of A* but never read it.[1] I daresay it's available in French. I haven't seen an English edition.

I haven't met A. Brookner—I'd like to very much & was to at a dinner party given by friends who know her, but she said at [the] last moment she couldn't come (I don't know why, but may be [an] ordinary good reason).[2] Hope to try again. I've met Timothy Mo, when I gave him a prize at a prize-giving gathering! He's perfectly sweet, along Vikram Seth lines, tho' different, being Chinese (or half Chinese).

Love & all best wish. I

1　*The Walnut Trees of Altenburg* (1943), a brilliant but little known novel by André Malraux.
2　Anita Brookner (born 1928), a rather reclusive English novelist and art historian, author of *Hotel du Lac* (1984).

DOI: 10.1057/9781137347909

68 HR OX2 Mar 3 [1988]

Dear Jeffrey,

Thanks for your letter. You seem to have bad luck with the Bayley books![1] How disgraceful those publishers are. John will raise the matter indignantly. Thank you for letting us know. Your Lawrence researches should bring up some interesting material.[2] Talking of his ex-mother-in-law, I met Al Alvarez just lately, at an Oxford party for Todorov * [in margin: he's an awfully nice chap] who came to give the Bateman lecture, and produced a good old-fashioned academic speech, to the disappointment of the young Turks.[3]

Re Verdi, I saw Jonathan Miller's modern dress Mafia *Rigoletto* lately, & found it *wonderful*.[4]

I'm glad your great fire damaged no one. One can't help being excited! All best wish & love. Iris

1   I'd tried in vain to get review copies of John's books.
2   Meyers, *D. H. Lawrence: A Biography* (NY: Knopf, 1990).
3   The English critic Al Alvarez (born 1929) married Frieda Lawrence's granddaughter (not daughter). Tzvetan Todorov (born 1939 in Bulgaria) writes opaque theoretical criticism in French. He was mercifully clear at Oxford.
4   The English author and physician, theater and opera director Jonathan Miller (born 1934) did brilliant versions of several Verdi operas.

68 Hamilton Rd Oxford [March 7, 1988]

Dear Jeffrey,

Thank you very much for letter and for sending the ad! We haven't heard of Dunstable College, but Dunstable is a town in Hertfordshire, and you might write to D.C., D. Herts. & see what happens.[1] I'm afraid I can't recall William Rose, except that he was very nice.[2] And (between you & me) I haven't read Richard Todd's book (glanced at it)—can't read books about myself.[3] I think he's a clever intelligent boy—also nice!

How delightful to see the deer! We used to have little muntjak deer sometimes in the Steeple Aston garden. We miss such things. At least we still have owls here. It sounds as if you are really discovering a new view of Lawrence. Hope to see you & Val over here—With love, Iris

1   I was trying to find Dr. M. S. Fisher who, as a child, had been taught by Lawrence. Dunstable is actually in Bedfordshire.

DOI: 10.1057/9781137347909

2   William Rose, an American professor, edited *The Letters of Wyndham Lewis* (1962) and wrote "Iris Murdoch, informally," *Shenandoah*, 19 (1968), 3–22.

3   Richard Todd, *Iris Murdoch* (London: Methuen, 1984).

68 Hamilton Rd Oxford [March 21, 1988]

Dear Jeffrey,

Thanks letter. I'll look out for traces of Dr. M. S. Fisher—I can probably think of some method. How awful to be tutored by D. H. Lawrence!

I did have a splendid fire in a novel I later abandoned. There's another fire in *The Italian Girl*.

I can imagine how many trials one has as editor of collections & anthologies etc! Stirring up the slow and getting politely rid of the bad!

Good news about your HOUSE—it sounds ideal—you will love arranging it. Very cheering. Excuse in haste, just going away (not for very long). Love & best wishes,

Iris

68 Hamilton Rd Oxford [March 29, 1988]

Dear Jeffrey,

Thank you for your letter.

I have not seen the *Vanity Fair* article (and don't want to).[1] Too bad we sound so drunk & decrepit. What a fascinating remark by Bowra![2] Ed Victor is my agent. I need one to prevent publishers underpaying me.[3] (I've only had an agent, i.e. Ed, for 2 or 3 years.)

John's book is absurdly priced because having no agent to advise him, he allowed it to be published by a disgraceful firm called Harvester Press.[4] They once published (republished) a book of mine on Sartre, the book was called *Sartre: Romantic Rationalist*. They produced a book entitled *Sartre: Romantic Realist*. On receiving a copy I pointed out this mistake. They apologised (vaguely), and I assumed they wd destroy all copies. They sold them all, and I am now credited in some lists with two different books!

Love & best wishes,

Iris

1   James Atlas, "The Abbess of Oxford," *Vanity Fair*, 51 (March 1988), 70, 76, 80, 82, 86. The title alludes to Muriel Spark's novel *The Abbess of Crewe* (1974).

DOI: 10.1057/9781137347909

2　Maurice Bowra (1898–1971), Oxford classical scholar, wit and well known homosexual, maliciously and quite absurdly said of Iris and John, "Lovely couple. I've slept with both of them."

3　Ed Victor raised her advances per novel from £10,000 to £50,000.

4　Bayley, *The Short Story*.

68 Hamilton Rd Oxford [May 4, 1988]

Dear Jeffrey,

Thank you for your letter with mention of raccoons. I'm glad you had a pleasant & rewarding Lawrence journey. I wonder if doctor M. S. Fisher was connected with the Fisher who was Warden of New College?[1] Yes, I daresay Lawrence was an inspiring teacher, I spoke out of prejudice![2] (I don't altogether like the personality of the author—yet I do like the poems, and *Kangaroo*. A genius of course & a lovely writer.) About Bowra's charming witticism—since you seemed in some doubt,—untrue of course. We were very fond of him & miss him. I hope you are enjoying plans for your new house. With love & best wishes, Iris

1　She was not related to Herbert Fisher (1865–1940), English historian and politician.

2　Despite her eminence and intellectual power, Iris was modest enough—when I challenged her—to admit that she was wrong about Lawrence.

[May 6, 1988]

Dear Jeffrey,

P.S. Your Honolulu letter has just come with new address. I posted a letter to your old address a day or two ago. I'm so glad you met Bob Martin, such a very nice chap.[1] I trust you've been enjoying Hawaii. We had a very lovely time there some years ago, with lots of *swimming*. John & I v. glad to hear about the Research Lectureship. All very best wishes for the new home, with love from,

Iris.

1　Robert Bernard Martin (1918–1999), the biographer of Hopkins, Tennyson and Edward FitzGerald, was teaching there.

DOI: 10.1057/9781137347909

68 Hamilton Rd Oxford [June 2, 1988]

Dear Jeffrey,

Thanks for your letter. Maui sounds a very nice place—I'd like to visit that vast scattering of islands. I hope the T. E. Lawrence gathering was interesting, and that you like him.[1] (Not everyone does.) I'm sorry to hear Jesus did not celebrate him.[2] Perhaps they now regard him as a dubious figure!

I expect you'll be over here this summer—let us know—all very best & love,

Iris

1   I've published three books on T. E. and certainly admire him.
2   Lawrence earned a first-class degree in history at Jesus College, Oxford University. Nineteen Eighty-Eight was the centenary of his birth.

68 HR OX2 Oct 1 [1988]

Dear Jeffrey,

Thanks very much for your letter of Sept 5 which I find here today after return from Italy, and *thanks* for interview. I have looked at it and I think it will take me a long time to check it—all minor things probably and rewording, but may need thought.[1] I return here to about 100 or so letters, some urgent. *Sorry* not to respond at once—will deal with interview before too long I hope. With love & best wishes,

Iris

[on envelope:] *Sorry* not send at once! See [Edward] Lear on stamp.

1   Though Iris did not read most writing about her, she took this *Paris Review* interview very seriously.

68 Hamilton Rd Oxford Oct 9 [1988]

Dear Jeffrey,

Sorry delay—I hope this reads OK! And sorry I couldn't fill out much, or in each case, where you suggested. I think it's probably still imperfect—my alterations may be inelegant etc—and I'd like to see a fair typescript for final polish. I hope that's OK too. (And I suppose I'll have

DOI: 10.1057/9781137347909

a proof.) I don't, at the moment, know what to do about the page of MS, but I expect I'll find something. I'll also go into the photo matter.

It's *beginning of term* and John feels daunted! I hope you are feeling full of fight! I much enjoyed our conversation. With love & best wishes,

Iris

68 Hamilton Rd Oxford Oct 31 [1988]

Dear Jeffrey,

Thanks for letter with account of your literary activity. Sorry I missed the lecture on Oct 10! How splendid that you have Alex de Jonge with you—do give him much love from John & me.[1] He is greatly missed in Oxford. I haven't met his wife whom he married (second marriage) shortly before leaving Oxford. I hope he *will* write more. He may have a fit of Slavic pessimism just at the moment.

About the interview—I *must* see a copy for correction—there was so much to change, and doing it on your original script looks rather confused, and I must see the typescript therefore in time, *before* it begins to be set up by the *Review*! I would *also* like to see the proofs. Must get it *right*. I haven't yet discovered a suitable "revised MS" page, but cd quickly do so. And I have given Chatto instructions about a photo. Shall I *send you* the photo and MS page? Or to *P. Review*?

We hope you will spend some sabbatical time in London—& *anyway* see you both here next summer.

With love, Iris

1   Alex De Jonge (born 1938), English biographer of Baudelaire, Peter the Great, Rasputin and Stalin, taught briefly at Colorado.

68 Hamilton Road Oxford November 14 [1988]

Dear Professor Kopff,[1]

I am glad to write to you in support of Professor Jeffrey Meyers who is applying for the post of Distinguished Professor. I have known Professor Meyers for a long time and have read many of his works. He is [a] very versatile and learned writer, whose books are widely studied and esteemed in academic circles in this country. He is a remarkable and lively scholar whose meticulous research, and deep appreciation

DOI: 10.1057/9781137347909

of literature, have inspired and enlightened a wide circle of readers. On many writers he is regarded as a prime authority. He is certainly a good candidate for the post in question.

With kind regards
Yours sincerely
Iris Murdoch

1   Christian Kopff of the Classics Department was leading my campaign for this position.

68 Hamilton Rd Oxford Nov 29 [1988]

Dear Jeffrey,

I'm glad you met Conradi, he's a good boy (& a Buddhist). Give my love to de Jonge if you see him. What a lovely cruise journey in store.¹ Sorry about the feminists who spoil the dinner parties.² (How? Couldn't they just come in pairs?)

I enclose a note of some small *alterations* which I would like to be made please on the text you sent me—which is mostly OK & beautifully typed! About the MS page. I am reluctant to send one from my current one, & enclose one from *The Book and the Brotherhood*. Does it matter being all crossed out? It looks a bit odd.

I've asked Chatto (Marian Covington) to send you a photo at once.

All very best wishes,
        Love I.

P.S. This, from the new not yet-published novel, might after all be better?

Love & best wishes, [in square box:] [I]

1   In December 1988 I lectured on my second Pearl cruise to Asia.
2   I blamed the feminists for the demise of the dinner party.

68 Hamilton Road Oxford Dec 24 [1988]

Dear Jeffrey,

I am amazed. Who do these *Paris Review* people think they are?¹ Are they French or Americans? Why do they think they're so grand? I thought they'd commissioned the thing? I'm not at all sure I want to answer their questions. It depends on what the questions are. You may

DOI: 10.1057/9781137347909

say that I will consider their questions. (Yes, I realize we have spent some time on this operation and it would be a pity to lose it!) I understand that there is no time limit. So much the better. I hope you didn't get too bored on the way to Bali.

With love and best New Year wishes, Iris

1   I interviewed Iris in July 1988, and the interview was published in the *Paris Review* in the summer of 1990. The ordeal with the journal was so unpleasant that I refused their offer to interview V. S. Naipaul, who would have been much more difficult to deal with.

68 Hamilton Rd OX2 7QA Jan 24 [1989]

Dear Jeffrey,

Thanks so much for your letter with travel and adventure news! Bali sounds lovely, and I'd like to see those ruins in Central Java. The Brazil-Argentine plan for next year sounds good, and your Berkeley summer.

I'm very sorry to hear about Francis King being so ill.[1] I knew about his friend's death.[2] What a terrible sequel. I rang his number two or three times in London at Christmas to ask him to a luncheon party & got no answer (perhaps just by accident). We spend Christmas in London—our London friends usually leave London at Christmas.

About the *Paris Review*—I was only being jokily ironical in my last letter. The bit of substance was that I was willing to look at their extra questions! I hope they have not got an impression of me as a sort of touchy grandee, which I am certainly not![3] I don't mind about the questions or when they publish. Perhaps you could let me have now the name & address of the editor so that I may make all that clearer?

We are having a wonderful warm sunny winter here, all the plants coming up & spring flowers to be seen. I'm glad you're having a mild winter too. As everyone here loves to say, we shall pay for it later! (But perhaps we won't, perhaps we've got away with it?) I lately read Kundera's *Unbearable Lightness* and liked it, and perhaps will try another of his.[4] I hope Lawrence goes on well. Good about the G. Greene book.[5]

With love & best wishes, I.

1   The English novelist Francis King (1923–2011), author of *Act of Darkness* (1983), was my close friend. He recovered from stomach cancer.
2   Francis' partner, the actor David Atkin, died in May 1988.

DOI: 10.1057/9781137347909

3   Iris' burst of irritation was most uncharacteristic. She had a gentle temperament and was certainly not (like Naipaul) a "touchy grandee."

4   Milan Kundera, Czech novelist (born 1929), published *The Unbearable Lightness of Being* in 1984.

5   Meyers, ed., *Graham Greene: A Revaluation* (London: Macmillan, 1990). John contributed an essay on Greene's short stories.

68 Hamilton Road Oxford Feb 25 [1989]

Dear Jeffrey,

Thanks very much for your letter. I'm afraid I did write a very quick note to *Paris Review* (some time before receiving your letter of Feb 19) to say I was glad to hear they were going to publish the piece, and that if they still wanted to ask questions I wd consider them. As they had definitely decided to publish, I thought an olive branch, or oil on water, move was in place. *I'm sorry*, and now wish I hadn't, and I do hope that won't delay things further— I feel pretty sure it won't. I haven't heard from them, and my note was vague and merely friendly! [In the margin: I can imagine they are far from efficient!] I'm sorry too I didn't answer your additional queries—I can't recall this exactly—I hope you are not cross with me, please say you are not.[1]

I read your Nobel prize piece with great interest and pleasure, and was amazed and thrilled and delighted when I reached the last sentence![2] How very kind of you to think of me here and utter those friendly generous thoughts. I am quite overcome. Thank you so much. And for such an interesting and informative article. I boast that I met a rarely seen winner of that prize, Halldór Laxness, in his remote snowbound house in Iceland.[3] We had a merry drunken time.

The Salman Rushdie business is absolutely horrifying.[4] Various declarations and pressure groups (e.g. international PEN) are setting up protests etc (I have signed one & expect others) but against the wicked awful power of Islam these moves, and even the disapproval etc of governments, can effect, it seems, nothing. One begins to have a nightmare of Islam conquering the planet in the next century.[5] That religion has, as well as its disregard of human life, another great advantage as it is the only creed which absolutely & fundamentally denies rights, even existence as human persons, to women! This must make it popular with the holders of power in innumerable countries!

I haven't seen reviews on *The Biographer's Art* but will look out for them.[6] We much look forward to the *Lawrence* and hope you have discovered those letters.[7]

DOI: 10.1057/9781137347909

I have finished a novel, called *The Message to the Planet*, [in the margin: published October perhaps,] in which the main characters are Jewish—rather a rash thing to do—a Jewish friend read it for me & said it sounded all right. I have removed one [or] two factual errors—e.g. I didn't know that if you give someone a prayer shawl it must be enclosed in its own special velvet bag! I am getting nowhere with thoughts of next novel at present.

Once more, I'm sorry about the *P. Review* matter and *apologize* for rushing in! I hope the piece will come out soon. With love and best wishes,

ever Iris

1 Iris revealed her characteristic sweetness and humility by apologizing for not originally agreeing to answer more questions and by worrying that I might be cross with her.

2 Meyers, "The Nobel Prize and Literary Politics," *Dictionary of Literary Biography Yearbook, 1988* (Columbia, S.C., 1989), pp. 188–192. I concluded by stating that Murdoch is "the most worthy and promising candidate for the Nobel Prize in Literature."

3 The Icelandic novelist Halldór Laxness (1902–1988) won the Nobel Prize in 1955.

4 Death threats, including a *fatwa* by the Ayatollah Khomeini of Iran, were made against Rushdie for his portrayal of Islam in *The Satanic Verses* (1988).

5 A shrewd prophecy in 1989.

6 Meyers, ed., *The Biographer's Art* (London: Macmillan, 1989).

7 Meyers, *D. H. Lawrence: A Biography* (NY: Knopf, 1990).

68 Hamilton Rd Oxford [March 22, 1989]

Dear Jeffrey,

Thank you very much for your letter which I was very glad to receive. And thanks for the offprint, always interesting. [vertical in margin: * *Thanks* for sending the Nobel piece on to the HQ!][1] We miss Marilyn Butler in Oxford—she has defected to Cambridge, as you know—I like both of them.[2] I greatly enjoy what I've heard & seen of Woody Allen—I find him very funny and also very touching. I've only seen one film, old one (Charlie Rose?) which I found good in parts, but have heard him on radio quite often.[3]

You seem to have a lot of jolly fine visitors in Boulder.[4] Brian Urquhart's mother taught at the noble left wing boarding school which I attended, and I think Brian was once a pupil in the junior school where a

DOI: 10.1057/9781137347909

few boys were allowed in![5] I've known him (a little) for ages, and admire him. Give him my best wishes.

My play based on *The Black Prince* is being put on at the Aldwych theatre in London opening 25 April. No great names in the cast, but an excellent actor, Ian McDiarmid, playing Bradley. I hope it will survive.

Hope DHL goes on well. Maybe we shall hear from *Paris Review* one day! With all best wishes & love, I

1   University professors are allowed to nominate candidates for the Nobel Prize in Literature. I nominated Iris, who certainly deserved it more than William Golding and Doris Lessing.

2   Marilyn Butler (born 1937), English literary critic, was Professor of English at Cambridge from 1986 to 1993.

3   Iris confused the American talk show host Charlie Rose (born 1942) with one of Woody Allen's minor movies *Broadway Danny Rose* (1984).

4   During my years in Boulder I was able to invite some notable lecturers and friends: William Chace, Frederick Crews, Denis Donoghue, Donald Greene and Frederick Karl.

5   Brian Urquhart (born 1919) was Undersecretary-General of the United Nations. Iris went to Badminton School in Bristol.

68 HR OX2 [received April 19, 1989]

Dear Jeffrey,

Thank you very much for your letter. I am very anxious about the play, which contains a number of soliloquies and some literary theorising. It also abruptly mixes funniness with sadness. There is a complex stage set with sofas moving on rails etc. The chief actor, Ian McDiarmid (not very well known) is marvellous however, and the love scenes (with 20 year old actress just out of drama school) are very touching (*I* think).[1] I saw it last night with a "pre-view" smallish audience & they seemed to intuit it alright. But I don't know how it will eventually "go over." Thanks for news & all best to Lawrence book,

with love, Iris

1   The young actress was Abigail Cruttenden (born 1969).

DOI: 10.1057/9781137347909

68 Hamilton Rd Oxford May 13 [1989]

Dear Jeffrey,

Thank you very much for your letter and the enclosure. I hope your many works go on very well! Please excuse enclosed in haste to bring some news of the play.[1] In spite of good notices I fear for it however, since the London Underground is now frequently on strike, and this deters theatre goers!

Perhaps the American tourists, like the cavalry, will arrive!

All best wishes & love, Iris

1   Iris sent a newspaper ad for the play, with excellent quotes from the critics.

Oxford June 7 [1989]

Dear Jeffrey,

Thanks very much letter and enclosure. DHL is a great writer but I don't (I confess) altogether like him. I like *Kangaroo* best, and some of the stories and poems. But I cannot love him and don't like his attitudes. I find Conrad a more congenial and possibly greater writer. I think *Lord Jim* is [a] wonderful novel. I read it again lately and was very deeply moved by it—including the later part which some say is less good.

About the *Daily Mail*—I gave no interview to the *Daily Mail*.[1] The first I heard of their article was when somebody said they'd seen it, and I got hold of a copy. The *Mail* never communicated with me or sent me a copy of the piece. Such are the ways of journalists. I *did* give an interview some time earlier to an American journalist, at the request of my agent Ed Victor, who recommended this man & said he would give a decent sober piece to a magazine called *People*.[2] The *Daily Mail* thing is partly based on that piece, partly on "investigative journalism." Some time before I received a letter from someone in Germany who said he was writing a life of Franz Steiner and could I say anything about him, memories of him etc, and I wrote him a letter which is, I am fairly sure, partly quoted verbatim in the *DM* article.[3] About Frank, there is a lot of general knowledge.[4] I can't imagine where the picture of Franz with me came from! The photo of John & me was taken by some journalist photographer, perhaps in connection with the *People*, I can't recall!

DOI: 10.1057/9781137347909

I hope you'll have a lovely time in the Berkeley Hills. It sounds very good for inspiration!

Love I.

Sorry about that chair. I'm sure you must be welcome in many other places.[5]

1   Sue Summers, "The Lost Loves of Iris Murdoch," *You Magazine: The Mail on Sunday*, June 5, 1988, pp. 16–22.

2   Ned Geeslin, with Fred Hauptfuhrer, "Iris Murdoch Is Britain's Prolific First Lady of Fiction," *People*, 29 (March 14, 1988), 125–126.

3   Franz Steiner (1909–1952), Czech ethnologist and linguist, taught at Oxford from 1950 to 1952. He was Iris' lover and inspired positive characters in three of her novels.

4   Frank Thompson, the great love of Iris' early life, was captured and executed in Bulgaria.

5   A host offered me a fragile chair which collapsed under me.

30 Charlbury Road Oxford OX2 6UU September 16 [1989]

Dear Jeffrey,

Thank you very much for letter and news of your summer and the *Paris Review*, animated at last. I've met Naipaul (nice chap) once or twice, but haven't read anything by him.[1] I think he'd be a splendid interviewee.

I envy you living with Conrad! (whom I *love*—I admire & respect D. H. Lawrence but do *not* love him!) The BBC has just decided to have *Lady Chatterley* read nightly as A Book at Bedtime, and this has occasioned an amusing fracas, and grave declarations (not always unreasonable) about the permissive society.[2]

We've been away in Devon, beside the sea, where it poured with rain, a cold wind blew, a damp mist concealed the landscape, and enormous waves dashed upon the shore precluding swimming. We are shortly going to Italy where we *hope* the summer is in continuous session. I'm glad you had such a nice time in Berkeley [in margin: & that you'll be in London next summer]—we have happy memories of that place! With love & best wishes,

yours, Iris

1   V. S. Naipaul, born in Trinidad in 1932, wrote *Guerrillas* (1975) and *A Bend in the River* (1979), and won the Nobel Prize in 2001. He was notoriously

DOI: 10.1057/9781137347909

nasty and very few would describe him as a "nice chap." Sometimes Iris, like Browning's Last Duchess, "smiled on all alike."

2   Lawrence's novel *Lady Chatterley's Lover*, was privately printed in Florence in 1928 and banned in Britain until a controversial trial in 1960 ruled that it was not obscene. Some people were alarmed that broadcasting this novel would lead to a sudden increase in fornication.

Tel (same) 0865-59483 30 Charlbury Rd OX2 6UU Oct 2 [1989]

Dear Jeffrey,

Much thanks [for] your letter full of cheerful news. We had a pleasant sunny hol in Italy, in Venice, then Padua and Mantua, looking at marvellous pictures & buildings. [in margin: hope you survived the "hike."] We also went to Bassano (near Alps) to see pix by painter of that name.¹ Venice remains magical & too-good-to-be-truish, & not too full of tourists at this time.

How splendid that you are doing le Carré's biography—a deep and most interesting subject—and that you'll interview Naipaul.² DHL in Montpellier should be interesting, and *delightful*, too. I note the (sad) anti-white-culture line taken by CF [Carlos Fuentes].³ This sort of ghetto sectionalism is so destructive. (There is a row here in the Labour Party about whether there should be something called "black sections.")

I heard about C. Sinclair-Stevenson's much lamented but entirely understandable departure from HH [Hamish Hamilton publishers].⁴ I'm afraid I don't know where he has gone. He took a lot of best chaps with him anyway!

We are just going (briefly since Ox Term is near) to Norway where a pupil of John's wants him to lecture. Au revoir & with love, I

1   Jacopo Bassano (c.1517–1992), Venetian painter.
2   Le Carré (born 1931) first encouraged and then blocked my proposed biography.
3   The Mexican novelist Carlos Fuentes (born 1928) had attacked European culture in a completely phony speech at Colorado.
4   The editor Christopher Sinclair-Stevenson (born 1939) published the English edition of my life of Katherine Mansfield in 1978. He briefly had his own publishing firm, then became a literary agent.

DOI: 10.1057/9781137347909

30 Charlbury Rd OX2 Oct 21 [1989]

Dear Jeffrey,

Thanks very much letter. In Venice we went to La Madonna too, led there by friends, yes very good![1] We enjoyed Oslo [in margin: Beautiful fjord, houses, paintings by Munch],[2] and went to the university at Tromsø, in the Arctic Circle. (Cold, not exceedingly, but snow expected. Fancy 3 months all dark, 3 months all light!)

Back in Oxford. No tennis here—you're lucky. I've also been to Dublin where all the writers talk to (and even with) each other. I like the sound of your Conrad articles—I never connected him with music—I'm glad he is proved not anti-Semitic.[3] I wish I could see an elk. I haven't any views on Sylvia Plath—I think I read some of her poems but can't remember.[4] I'll get my publisher to send you copy of novel.[5] (Lots of Jews in it.) With love, I

1   La Madonna, hidden away down an alley near the Rialto bridge and famous for *zuppa di pesce*, is an excellent restaurant in Venice.

2   Edvard Munch (1863–1944) was the Norwegian Expressionist painter of *The Scream* (1893).

3   Meyers, "Conrad and Music," *Conradiana*, 23 (Autumn 1991), 179–195.

4   Sylvia Plath (1932–1963), American novelist and poet, author of *The Bell Jar* (1963) and *Ariel* (1966).

5   Murdoch, *The Message to the Planet* (1989).

30 Charlbury Rd OX2 [November 10, 1989]

Dear Jeffrey,

How splendid you will be with Murray for those two very interesting books![1] I *adore* Conrad. (*Lord Jim* is *his best*, I read it at school & reread it at intervals, it sheds such *light!*) I met le Carré but only momentarily [in margin: he certainly seemed very nice], and have nothing to communicate about him. I had lunch with Leonard Woolf at the Athenaeum and liked him a lot.[2]

I hope your football team won. No knowledge of V. Greene.[3] All very best wishes and with love, I

1   Meyers, *Joseph Conrad: A Biography* (London: John Murray, 1991) and *Edgar Allan Poe: His Life and Legacy* (London: John Murray, 1992). Murray was Byron's publisher and remained in the same nineteenth-century offices.

DOI: 10.1057/9781137347909

2 Leonard Woolf (1880–1969), English political theorist and autobiographer, was the husband of Virginia Woolf. The Athenaeum is a handsome and venerable London club.

3 Vivien Greene (1904–2003), the long-separated wife of the Catholic novelist Graham Greene.

30 Charlbury Rd OX2 [January 1990]

Dear Jeffrey,

Thanks so much for your letter. San Diego must have been lovely—we were there once briefly. (Tho' we failed to go to the picture gallery and did not know till later how good it is—it contains a picture by Luini which I've been trying to track for years. We have a splendid copy of it.)[1] We were mainly with the fishes (when not, of course, at the University).

I'm glad you are doing the *7 Pillars* introduction. I *love* T. E. Lawrence, who seems to be *hated* by many people here.[2] (I also *detest* D. H. Lawrence, the chap not his books, who seems to be *worshipped* by many people here!)

Best of luck to Rachel in her university search. I hope Val has had a fast and very ok and painless time in hospital—it is good when any such thing is *over* and one feels liberated. Sorry short letter. I am *overwhelmed* by mail after Christmas and because I (very unusually) have been on TV lately.

All very best wishes, and love to Val, and to Rachel, and to you,

[in box:] [I]

1 Bernardino Luini (c.1481–1532) was a North Italian painter influenced by Leonardo da Vinci.

2 Richard Aldington's *T. E. Lawrence: A Biographical Enquiry* (1955) damaged Lawrence's reputation, but he is still admired as the greatest hero of World War I and the author of a masterpiece, *Seven Pillars of Wisdom* (1926).

30 Charlbury Rd OX2 [March-April 1990]

Dear Jeffrey,

Thanks so much for letter with Conrad and DHL news. Blessed Conrad, a truly spiritual man. And good news about Rachel, with her interesting choice of universities. I've heard about Harbourfront, they invited me but I couldn't come.[1] I am in general rather off journeys. I enjoyed the one to New York however, and was able to see the Met & Frick pictures. (Some new dinky skyscrapers as well.)

DOI: 10.1057/9781137347909

We look forward to seeing you in London in August. With all v. best wishes & love,

[I]

1   I spoke three times at the Harbourfront International Writers Festival in Toronto, and saw J. F. Powers in Minnesota on the way back.

30 Charlbury Road OX2 [April 1990]

Dear Jeffrey,

Much thanks your letter. I've been away (in Spain) and am about to go away again—why does one do it (go away)?[1] Staying at home and working quietly is much jollier!

I'm glad you had a good time in lovely Berkeley. About biographies—I can't think—John Cowper Powys? Marvellous writer. But he wrote his own voluminous biography.[2] Andrew's biography goes slowly—there is so little to tell.[3] We hope to see you in summer. With love & best wishes, Iris

1   Iris did not remain "rather off journeys" for very long.
2   I had asked Iris for ideas about a new biographical subject. The British novelist John Cowper Powys (1872–1963) published his *Autobiography* in 1934.
3   A. N. Wilson, unfortunately, never wrote his biography of Iris, of whom there was a very great deal to tell.

[late April 1990]

Dear Jeffrey,

I'm so pleased to hear the news about Rachel—you must all be so happy—give her my very best wishes![1]

In Spain, we were in Galicia where it rained and John got food poisoning, otherwise OK!

Glad to hear of DHL biog, and (we hope) *Paris Review* active at last! With all best wishes & love,

Iris

1   Rachel was accepted at Swarthmore College in Pennsylvania.

DOI: 10.1057/9781137347909

30 Charlbury Rd OX2 Sept 11 [1990]

Dear Jeffrey,

Much thanks for your letter of Sept 4. It was a great treat to see you and Val—and I hope next time to see Rachel too. I hope she is getting on well. Your DHL has had splendid reviews. Sorry about *Paris Review*. They seem to be absolutely first class muddlers. I'm glad you salvaged some.[1] All the best for Scott Fitzgerald (a lively subject!).[2] I hope you have by now waded far into that mountain of letters.

Literary note: Someone digging into my mother's (née Richardson) family tree (from 1619 when they were granted an estate in Co. Tyrone & a coat of arms) has found out that Henry Handel Richardson was a cousin of my grandfather![3]

Love & best wishes to you both,

Iris

1   Meyers, "An Interview with Iris Murdoch," *Denver Quarterly*, 26 (Summer 1991), 102–111.
2   Meyers, *Scott Fitzgerald: A Biography* (NY: HarperCollins, 1994).
3   Henry Handel Richardson (1870–1946) was an Australian woman novelist and author of *The Getting of Wisdom* (1910).

[September 17, 1990]

Dear Jeffrey,

In haste. I've just received your text of the interview (interesting stuff I think), but would like to *amend* it & *add* to it in [a] number of *minor* ways—so could it be held?

~~Amazing~~ Amusing literary point—(discovered by someone studying my mother's family tree): the woman novelist Henry Handel Richardson was a second cousin of my grandfather.

With love & best wishes,

Iris

30 Charlbury Road Oxford [October 1990]

Dear Jeffrey,

Please excuse a short note. I am rather overwhelmed by requests, tasks and obligations! I'm glad about *Lawrence*, I see it praised everywhere.

DOI: 10.1057/9781137347909

And about Rachel enjoying Swarthmore—that's very good! I haven't been to Harbourfront, tho' was invited.

I haven't read Boyd or Ford.[1]

It is beginning of term, never a jolly time for John! However it is *raining* at last after the driest summer on record.

Be well,

with love, I

It was lovely to see you in London!

1   William Boyd, English novelist born in 1952, is the author of *A Good Man in Africa* (1981) and *An Ice-Cream War* (1982). Richard Ford, American novelist born in 1944, is the author of *The Sportswriter* (1986) and *Independence Day* (1995).

30 Charlbury Road OX2 [November 5, 1990]

Dear Jeffrey,

Much thanks for your letter. I'm glad you had such a splendid time at Harbourfront with lots of interesting people. I only met Ackroyd once, but I instantly liked him very much.[1] I haven't been in touch with Andrew [Wilson] just lately, but I haven't heard about his giving up the biography. Perhaps there is so little to say! About E. A. Poe, I haven't read much of him—but he seems to be a remarkable writer in his own genre. J. F. Powers sounds nice. I have just read *Karamazov*, and will return to Proust. Sun shines here, have a lovely autumn. With love, I

1   Peter Ackroyd (born 1949), English novelist and biographer, wrote lives of T. S. Eliot, Dickens, Blake and Thomas More.

[January 18, 1991]

Dear Jeffrey,

Much thanks letter—I hope you had a lovely sunny time in California. We had a little snow. Now we have snowdrops in flower. I don't think any *Lucky Jim* character was based on me—I never heard this before![1] When LJ was written I scarcely knew Kingsley, and had published nothing

DOI: 10.1057/9781137347909

myself [in margin: except perhaps the *Sartre* book], so it's unlikely![2] I'm glad to [hear] our interview has found a home. Be well—don't work *too* hard! Keep in touch. Ever,

with love from Iris

1 Kingsley Amis' comic novel *Lucky Jim* was published in 1954.
2 Murdoch, *Sartre: Romantic Rationalist* (1953).

30 Charlbury Rd OX2 [March 11, 1991]

Dear Jeffrey,

Much thanks for two letters. We don't know yet about the Warton Chair.[1] I'll let you know! I was surprised by the ST [*Sunday Times*] statement. I was not in the least embarrassed by Andrew's questions! (What nonsense journalists invent!)[2] He is an old friend (pupil of John's) and we have known him well for 25 years. He has not given up the biography. He is used to doing a lot of different things at once.

Let me know about your summer plans. Spring has definitely broken out here! I have been in Paris looking at pictures. I hope Rachel is enjoying college. With love & best wishes,

Iris.

1 I'd asked about John's successor as Warton Professor of English at Oxford.
2 *Sunday Times* (London), February 17, 1991: "it has been said that Murdoch was pained by the embarrassing over-familiar questions Wilson once put to her on a television interview."

30 Charlbury Rd OX2 [March 11, 1991]

P.S. John's successor in the Warton Chair is Terry Eagleton.[1]

What super news about your going to Berkeley![2] A splendid move, you must feel very happy. A lovely place, lovely houses, lovely people!

Love & best wishes,

[I]

& thanks re *Conrad* Biography.

DOI: 10.1057/9781137347909

Look forward read!
I love Conrad.

1   Terry Eagleton (born 1943), influential literary theorist, is the very antithesis of John Bayley. Eagleton taught at Oxford for ten years, then moved on to Manchester and Lancaster.
2   In June 1992, after teaching for thirty years I went back to Berkeley and became a professional writer.

[March 11, 1991]

Further P.S.

I have just gathered that the news of the next holder of the Warton Chair has not yet been publicly released! So *please do not mention it* to anyone! I will let you know when it is "out"!

With love & best wishes,

Iris

[March 12, 1991]

I think the TE [Terry Eagleton] decision is now generally known. Do you read his books? It is an interesting choice.[1]

When are you going to Berkeley? Many Oxonians are there, it is a favourite place!

All best wishes & love, I

1   After being over-scrupulous about the disclosure of news, Iris was now terribly discreet about the literary theorist whose work she heartily disliked.

30 Charlbury Rd OX2 6UU [March 22, 1991]

Dear Jeffrey,

Thanks for your letter. John of course had nothing to do with the choice of his successor. Our views about the latter coincide with yours! We, and many others, were surprised and horrified. I'm sorry about what the ST [*Sunday Times*] said—we certainly did not intend to sell our presentation copies of AW [Andrew Wilson]. We keep all such. We received several

DOI: 10.1057/9781137347909

copies of the book on publication, and must have for once set aside the wrong one for sale. I regret that very much. There is no end of the spite of journalists.[1]

What a splendid find, that descendant of Poe, with all that new material![2] Let me know about your visit. We look forward to Conrad. We have met and like Denis Donoghue, but do not know him well—he is indeed a merry fellow.

With love & best wishes, I

1   Iris liked everyone but journalists, Islamic fundamentalists and the IRA.
2   I found and had an illuminating interview with Edgar Allan Poe III.

30 Charlbury Rd OX2 [April 10, 1991]

Dear Jeffrey,

Many thanks for letter and Poe news. P must be a very interesting subject—and not much in view at present. And glad to hear of Rachel's progress and Happiness. We look forward to the *Conrad*.

Now what *does Commem* Commemorate?[1] I imagine it is just a salute to the great past of the great college in question—also of course ex-members of the college may turn up. You must be looking forward to your 1½ years in Europe—and not only in UK—such a splendid idea & prospect. I have a novel but am not working on it at present—just doing a little philosophy for once. (Too difficult—) With love & best wishes, I

Lovely spring here, flowers everywhere--

1   Commem Week, which takes place at the end of the academic year at Oxford, commemorates the benefactors of the university. It is celebrated with a sermon, a ceremony with oration, a garden party, a ball and considerable drunken revelry.

30 Charlbury Rd OX2 [July 22, 1991]

Dear Jeffrey,

Much thanks your letter! I'm sorry I didn't write sooner. I have been away, briefly in France, then in the North of England. [in margin: Cold, swam in sea.] How splendid that you will be living in Berkeley—and

DOI: 10.1057/9781137347909

what fun to choose a House among all those beautiful residences! And hordes of *very nice* intellectuals!

I believe that you will be in London later this summer? I hope it's not a dream. I am reading John Cowper Powys—I like him very much. And also Zola. I loved *Germinal* but cannot get on with *L'Assommoir*.[1]

Be well, send news of houses, and Europe visit. With love, I

1   The French naturalistic novelist Emile Zola (1840–1902) wrote *Germinal* (1885), about a coalminers' strike in northern France, and *L'Assommoir* (*The Dram Shop*, 1877), about alcoholism and poverty in working-class Paris.

30 Charlbury Road OX2 [late August 1991]

Dear Jeffrey,

Much thanks for your letter. What a super house you have in Berkeley—that paradise! And what adventures you have had in the summer (well, it's still summer I suppose—a bit cold here now.) John hasn't retired yet—he retires next June. He is looking forward to it! He has received the Conrad book and *loves* it! It has had indeed very good reviews (thanks for enclosure)—unfortunately he was not asked to review it, he would have been very glad to praise it—he has kept on reading me pieces of it! I haven't got hold of it yet. Now on with Poe! I envy your hot spring-cold spring experience! We only swim in the Thames. With love & best wishes,

ever I

30 Charlbury Rd Oxford OX2 [September 9, 1991]

Dear Jeffrey,

Thanks for your news of adventures (780 miles in one day!)—and of books (E. A. Poe ready soon.) You must be settling into lovely Berkeley now—not so far from Strawberry Creek (I hope that's right). I hope that architect is looking after your books. Amazing warm dry weather here— *too much*. Excuse a brief letter as we are just going (not for long) to Italy, where it will be even hotter & even drier (dryer?).

DOI: 10.1057/9781137347909

I forget if you like John Cowper Powys—I do. At any rate we have been swimming in the Thames.

With love & best wishes,

Iris

30 Charlbury Rd OX2 6UU [October 8, 1991]

Dear Jeffrey,

Thanks for your letter. What a delightful routine you have—and especially *swimming*! I remember Black Oak—I'm glad your reading went well there.[1] We had a pleasant time in Italy—Naples, Amalfi, Ravello, Salerno, Sorrento, even Capri. I say even Capri, because we expected it to be so full of tourists. It *was* so full of tourists, but somehow delightful all the same. Our north Italian friends, who think the Mafia begins at Bologna, said we would certainly be robbed, but we weren't. (I even bought a money-belt just in case.) We saw the great Greek temples at Paestum.[2] I expect you know this coast.

We look forward to seeing you in London next year. I'm glad you have this lovely house in Berkeley. Very best wishes to you all, and love & from John,

Iris

1   Black Oak was an excellent bookstore in North Berkeley.
2   Paestum is about fifty miles southeast of Naples.

[October 8, 1991]

Jeffrey dear,

P.S. thank you very much for sending the *Denver Quarterly* with our interview—and thank you for the interview! I think, actually, it's jolly good! All your doing.

With lots of love, I

DOI: 10.1057/9781137347909

30 Charlbury Rd OX2 [November 8, 1991]

Dear Jeffrey,

Thanks for your letter. We shall look forward to Poe! I haven't read anything by Nadine Gordimer, though I have met her and much liked her.[1] I don't know Lurcock [in margin: There are some Lurcooks as well], but the Oxford telephone directory lists an A. F. T. Lurcock at 9 Monmouth Rd, Oxford. That seems promising.

I'm glad Rachel is happy and looking forward! It's beautiful autumn here too, no frosts, tho' the temperature must be lower than yours.

We are hoping for some compromise in Madrid.[2] (Israelis, Palestinians)—it is all so sad—

I belong to an Anglo-Spanish group of thinkers (economists, politicians & some of us culture persons) which meets every year, in Spain or England—the question of Gibraltar was raised several years ago, but then it was decided to give it up (passions were rising)![3] We had another go (in the political group) this year. Again no use! ~~At least we're out~~ With love & best wishes,

Iris

1   The South African novelist Nadine Gordimer (born 1923), author of *The Late Bourgeois World* (1966) and *Burger's Daughter* (1979), won the Nobel Prize in 1991.
2   The Madrid Conference of October 1991, sponsored by the United States and the Soviet Union, failed to start a peace process between Israel and Palestine.
3   Gibraltar, an important naval base on the southwest coast of Spain and at the entrance to the western Mediterranean, is ruled by Britain and hotly claimed by Spain.

30 Charlbury Rd OX2 Dec 23 [1991]

Dear Jeffrey,

Much thanks letter, excuse late reply, what with *Christmas* and having a sort of 'flu. Getting better now. I hope you have had a happy Christmas in Austin—what a strange wonderful city of buildings the University is! I'm glad about your tennis. I swim when I can—but that's less & less often. I wish I had a private pool! No, I haven't been to Malta or Cyprus. However I *have* been (though often not for long) to Iceland, Canada, USA, Turkey, Egypt, Morocco, China, Japan, Thailand, Lebanon, Singapore, Cambodia (I got to Angkor before Pol Pot), Australia, New Zealand, Korea, Mexico, India, Israel; *not* South America, and *not* Africa except north coast.[1] I wish I'd been to Burma.[2]

DOI: 10.1057/9781137347909

Thank you v. much for the interesting and lively interview. I saw Norman Mailer in London at a party for his book—I like him a lot but hardly ever see him.[3]

Be well, near your stream, in 1992.

With love, I

1   Angkor Wat is the series of Khmer temples in the Cambodian jungle. Pol Pot (1925–1998), genocidal leader of the Khmer Rouge, killed millions of people, about 20 percent of the Cambodian population, between 1976 and 1979.

2   I trumped Iris by visiting all these countries (except Iceland and Lebanon) and traveling extensively in South America and Africa.

3   Norman Mailer (1923–2007), American novelist and essayist, author of *The Naked and the Dead* (1948) and *Armies of the Night* (1968).

30 Charlbury Rd OX2 [January 27, 1992]

Dear Jeffrey,

You have been having a marvellous journey! I do like Santa Barbara, but I was rather disappointed with New Orleans. I found the French Quarter rather tame & shabby— and I had also expected to see the Delta of the Mississippi! (No good—actually I think it doesn't exist. The great river was very undramatic at N.O.) And we didn't get to the alligators. Your class sounds very nice. John's finished Housman (not to be out for a while yet) and is writing reviews and teaching students, he is very pastoral.[1] He looks forward to next June.

Rather cold here, no snowdrops.

With love, I

1   Bayley, *Housman's Poems* (Oxford: Clarendon, 1992).

30 Charlbury Road OX2 [February 19, 1992]

Dear Jeffrey,

Thanks so much for your letter and always welcome news of your adventures! And perhaps Rachel will come to Somerville! my old college—now in a state of turmoil because at last the governing body have decided to admit MEN! A great storm is raging. The undergraduates (junior common room) are, almost to a woman, *absolutely opposed*, and the college is decked with big red posters & banners saying [in a

DOI: 10.1057/9781137347909

square box:] NO! I am on their side. I enjoyed Somerville & St. Anne's life without botheration by males, one could easily meet them anyway, the creatures are all over the place. I fear however that economic reasoning and the will of history will prevail![1]

Love & best wishes,
Ever I.

Looking forward to seeing Rachel at Oxford.

1   History prevailed and the first male students were admitted in 1994.

30 Charlbury Road OX2 [mid-May 1992]

Dear Jeffrey,

Many thanks letter. I am very sorry, I don't know of anyone with a flat to rent—and we are using ours at regular intervals, so no good. *So sorry*—We have a deafening dawn chorus too, but no mocking birds! This in haste with all best wishes & love—do hope you will find a place,

Iris

Hope you get the Berkeley house—lovely place to live!

30 Charlbury Rd OX2 [summer 1992]

Dear Jeffrey,

Thank so much letter and so glad to hear of your fine new house with view of two bridges, and in *Kensington*, a very *select* part of town! It sounds altogether ideal. Yes, we met Wendy (introduced as Freddie's daughter) at his wedding to Dee Wells. [in margin: No, we didn't know of her existence beforehand. V. nice girl!][1] We were the only witnesses. Let us know when you're in London. We shall be away in August but only v. briefly. I am still rather exhausted after the bout of bronchitis, and can't work very well. Yes, Poe has just arrived, many thanks—and all the best to Fitzgerald.

With love and from John,
                    Iris

1   Wendy Fairey is the daughter of the Oxford philosopher A. J. (Freddie) Ayer and, most improbably, Sheilah Graham, the Hollywood columnist and last lover of Scott Fitzgerald.

DOI: 10.1057/9781137347909

30 Charlbury Rd OX2 [late October 1992]

Dear Jeffrey,

Thanks very much for your letter with news of your French adventures! We haven't been doing anything to boast about, except worry about the future of Europe. (And who will be president of USA.)[1] My *Metaphysics* book has been published here at last, and will be published in USA (Viking, Dawn Seferian etc) in December or January I think. I'm glad you are getting on well with Fitz and have talked with V. Naipaul.[2] We shall be going to Spain to do a job for the British Council and look forward to visiting the Prado.

We've lately been to Cheltenham, where John gave the annual Shakespeare lecture, and to Norwich where I talked about philosophy. (I have *had enough* of philosophy for the present!)

I love your address![3]

Lots of love to you all and from J, I

1   Bill Clinton defeated the incumbent George H. W. Bush and became president.
2   I had been corresponding and talking on the phone to Vidia Naipaul for a decade. In August 1992 we finally met at his house in Wiltshire and his flat in London, and I was briefly anointed his authorized biographer.
3   My Olde Englishe address is: Stratford Road, Kensington.

[St. Catherine's College letterhead crossed out.] 30 Charlbury Rd OX2 [November 17, 1992]

Dear Jeffrey,

Much thanks yr letter and for the interesting Conrad piece.[1] You are as busy as ever *and* you can swim in the Pacific with the seals! How I long to swim with seals! I saw some off the Scottish coast 3 years ago— they are such darlings. I have, with John, been in Spain [in margin: I'm interested that you lived there for so long] giving lectures or discussions in Madrid, Santiago and Salamanca. I feel rather at home in Spain, though our Spanish has rusted. I was inclined to cheer Clinton, however it seems [in margin: from newspaper here] he has been hi-jacked by Irish-Americans, is demanding that Britain should "use less lethal force" in Ulster, and says that Gerry Adams (head of Sinn Fein) could visit America on a fund-raising tour! He apparently doesn't mention the IRA. (The "funds" are for terrorists of course.) Also he indicates that he will

DOI: 10.1057/9781137347909

resist the extradition of suspected terrorists. Well, well. Perhaps someone will jog his elbow.

What lovely trees you have in your garden, and covered in leaves & flowers. Winter begins here, the leaves are falling and fallen. Soon Christmas cards will be on show! Love to you all, and from John, ever I

1   Meyers, "Conrad and Jane Anderson: An Unknown Letter," *Conradiana*, 24 (Autumn 1992), 235–236.

[St. Catherine's College letterhead crossed out.] [November 20, 1992]

Jeffrey, P.S. about your Murdoch "collected writings" book.[1] I like the idea—I'm not sure what it should include. I'd like to put in my (only) short story, some poems, an article (my earliest publication I think) in the *Aristotelian Society* (entitled *Nostalgia for the Particular*—pre-Derrida etc!)[2] I will try to think of other items—there may not be enough, however.

Love & best wishes,

Iris

Include *Acastos, Sovereignty of Good* & *The Fire & the Sun*?[3] Problems with the publishers?[4]

1   I wanted to edit a *Viking Portable Iris Murdoch*.
2   Iris published a book of poems, *A Year of Birds*, in 1978. "Nostalgia for the Particular" appeared in *Proceedings of the Aristotelian Society*, 52 (1952), 243–260. This was her earliest publication in philosophy. Jacques Derrida (1930–2004), an influential French philosopher, developed the literary theory of deconstruction.
3   Murdoch's three books of philosophy were published respectively in 1986, 1970 and 1977.
4   She means problems securing permission to reprint from different publishers.

30 Charlbury Road Oxford OX2 6UU March 4 [1993]

Dearest Jeffrey,

I hope you are well and I *do* hope you are not cross with me, as I don't think I have heard from you for quite a long time.[1] I hope you are not cross about the business of collecting essays etc (which I am still not

DOI: 10.1057/9781137347909

doing). As for my biography Andrew said he would pick it up again, but when I met him lately he did not mention it. I do rather hope this matter can be postponed until I have left the scene. I have asked Viking to send you a copy of my philosophy book.[2] I felt rather paralysed about it and imagined it would get little attention, either in England or in America, but it seems to have been noticed.

About Clinton (I mentioned this to you earlier) sending an envoy to Ulster to solve the Irish question! Our idiotic prime minister seems to have allowed this to take place.[3] The aim apparently is to study problems of "abuse of human rights." This is certainly surprising, as between two sovereign states! A visit to Dublin, mentioning (not I think mentioned) the IRA, might be more useful. I feel less hostile to Clinton now that I have been told that his mother was née Kelly.

My next novel, *The Green Knight* (connected with *Sir Gawain and the Green Knight*) should come out perhaps in October.[4] I am now very much at a loss, unable to conjure up any new scene. So I am a bit depressed. Pray do not be cross with me, but send some news of yourself.

With much love,

Iris

1   I was never cross with Iris, merely waiting for her response to my last letter.
2   Murdoch, *Metaphysics as a Guide to Morals* (1992).
3   The Conservative John Major was prime minister from 1990 to 1997.
4   *Sir Gawain and the Green Knight* is a late fourteenth-century Arthurian alliterative poem.

30 Charlbury Rd OX2 [late March 1993]

Dear Jeffrey,

I am so sorry to have failed to reply to a letter. I usually reply rather promptly, but must have missed this one, *sorry*. [vertically in margin: Perhaps the letter went to the wrong address? Perhaps this one is going there too!]

I do admire your energy. I am feeling rather exhausted at the moment. I forget if I told you, my next novel is to be out here in October (I think), called *The Green Knight* (N.B. *Sir Gawain and*)

John has read and very much enjoyed your POE book, and I will soon have it too. Now for *Fitzgerald*—410 pages in 4 months—I cd *never* manage that. You are a great power house.

DOI: 10.1057/9781137347909

Edmund Wilson next. I recall meeting him* [in margin: *with John] in Oxford I *think* chez Isaiah Berlin, in a dark room.[1] He was rather tough & forbidding and he frightened me. I think Mary McCarthy was with him, or perhaps I dreamed that.[2] I hope your Poe film will come off and the riches will materialize. My friend Josephine Hart has had a hair-raising film made of her first novel *Damage* (excellent title).[3] Poe should be a great subject! I hope Rachel is enjoying the university scene.

I'm glad Clinton is turning out well. Our politicians are in total confusion, even chaos! Poor old Europe, poor old Russia, poor old Britain, poor old Ireland. (I am going to receive an honorary degree in Ulster.)

I hope you had lovely time in Santa Barbara, lovely place. (Very good fish restaurant.)

Much love,

ever Iris

1   Edmund Wilson (1895–1972), author of *Axel's Castle* (1931) and *To the Finland Station* (1942), was the leading American man of letters in the twentieth century. Isaiah Berlin (1909–1997) was an eminent Oxford philosopher and historian of ideas.

2   The American novelist Mary McCarthy (1912–1989), author of *The Groves of Academe* (1952) and *The Group* (1962), was married to Wilson from 1938 to 1946.

3   Josephine Hart (1942–2011), born in Ireland, published *Damage* in 1991. The film of the same name was directed by Louis Malle and released in 1992.

30 Charlbury Rd OX2 [April 24, 1993]

Dearest Jeffrey,

Much thanks letter. As I think I told you Josephine has a film offer for her second book, and is writing her third book.[1] She has a wild Irish passionate dark soul which lends itself well to literature. I haven't got very far with anything. I was briefly in Spain at Alcala, where I saw beautiful storks building their nests.[2] I have been to Wales and stayed at a pub called *The Green Man*. (We, I should say, John drove the car!) There is lovely country out there, and mountains (hills). My novel is not going very well (I mean the one I am trying to write). I am developing a sort of bronchitis. I hope Rachel is finding a good summer adventure in the radio & TV world. Hemingway's Irish daughter-in-law must be an interesting (also wild) girl.[3] Apropos Ireland & the Catholic Church, now that the Church of England is admitting *women priests*, remarkably

DOI: 10.1057/9781137347909

large numbers of it are going *over to Rome*! This is dreadful! (I am very glad about women priests.) Excuse short letter. I am really feeling rather ill—but will have recovered soon I have no doubt.

Much love to you, I

1   Josephine Hart's second novel was *Sin* (1992), her third was *Oblivion* (1995).
2   Alcalá de Henares, a university town and birthplace of Cervantes, is about twenty miles northeast of Madrid.
3   Valerie Danby-Smith (born 1940), Hemingway's secretary, later married and divorced his youngest son, Gregory.

30 Charlbury Rd OX2 [May 17, 1993]

Jeffrey dear,

Much thanks letter. I'm so glad to hear of Rachel's splendid success, beating all the others. Also to hear that you have a good agent now. I find Ed V[ictor] very good, getting me more than my old thoughtless arrangements with Chattos! Your new walks also sound attractive, including the cemetery.

I haven't much news. I think I told you I have a novel, *The Green Knight*, coming out in October here, I think Jan in US. (It has some relation to Sir Gawain!) I am trying to begin another novel but cannot so far. (Perhaps it is time to stop juggling, and fall off the high wire. I hope not however!) John & I are just going to Japan for 2-3 weeks (we've been twice before but not lately) where we hope we will suitably entertain the Japanese, and see some pleasant sights and ancient things.

I hope you'll be over here this summer? Well, it is really summer now, & the trees & flowers are lovely. Much love, I

30 Charlbury Rd OX2 [June 16, 1993]

Dear Jeffrey,

Many thanks for your letter. How splendid of you to spend a year in Japan really *learning* about the place, however awful![1] You should write *your* biography. Why not? I have written to Ed Victor about W. H. Allen and to Chatto about UK rights.[2] I'm afraid I haven't heard of Abner Stein.[3] One or two mannerisms of Julius may resemble some of Kreisel, but in general character there is no resemblance.[4] (Kreisel is an old and dear friend of mine.)

DOI: 10.1057/9781137347909

I am now in wild Derbyshire, on the annual tour arranged by John's two elder brothers! Excuse brief letter. We keep moving on from place to place. John is interested to hear of J. Frank.[5] He hasn't got a copy of his *Observer* review, but cd probably find one. (My Mont Blanc fountain pen has just given up and I have forgotten to bring any ink!)

With all best wishes & love, I

[on envelope:] P.S. and thanks very much for the O'Brian cutting![6]

1   In 1965–966 I taught air force personnel for the University of Maryland in Okinawa, Japan and Korea.

2   W. H. Allen is a British publisher.

3   Abner Stein, an English agent, was connected to my American agent.

4   Georg Kreisel (born 1923), Austrian-Jewish mathematical logician, was taught and respected by Ludwig Wittgenstein. Julius King is a character in *A Fairly Honourable Defeat* (1970).

5   Joseph Frank (1918–2013), a friend who taught nearby at Stanford, was the author of the acclaimed five-volume biography of Dostoyevsky. John, an expert in Russian literature, reviewed the second volume.

6   Iris admired the popular English novelist Patrick O'Brian (1914–2000), author of *Master and Commander* (1969).

30 Charlbury Rd OX2 6UU [July 5, 1993]

Dear Jeffrey,

Thank you very much for your letter. I am so sorry to hear of your awful time in Japan (this would be of great interest to your autobiography). A detail—the howling dogs—they still howl—the Japanese still tie them up. The whole scene was much brighter and happier & more humane than in our previous 2 visits. Their technology is beautiful—make an island by removing a complete mountain top—span miles & miles of islands with bridges in a few years—and as for the trains, very long, 150 mph, absolutely accurate with time, stopping at stations with doors exactly opposite to the same number on the platform (etc). Everyone we met very calm & very friendly.

I am glad you heard from Isaiah—he is a noble letter-writer—and that Wilson is proceeding.[1] I have just been in Ireland, Ulster, University of Coleraine, to receive an hon. degree. It was a happy time, I met with my cousins who live in Belfast, but came to Coleraine to see me. We used to swim together in those wild waves when we were children. Such a

DOI: 10.1057/9781137347909

beautiful coastline. How I wish Oxford could be removed to be by the sea. Maybe the Japanese cd do it.

I am very so very sorry to hear of the recent death of your younger brother—

I hope you will have good travels. With love & best wishes,

ever Iris

1   I interviewed Isaiah Berlin, a friend of Edmund Wilson, at the Athenaeum club in London.

30 Charlbury Rd OX2 [August 1993]

Dear Jeffrey,

So glad to hear of your many travels and adventures. We have, after Japan, been more sober, exploring Wiltshire, Herefordshire, and Dorset. You are bold and brave and *deserve* to be sailing and canoeing and *swimming*. (Ah, swimming—I have been in the sea once this year.) I don't know when you'll get this—it is also to say, re publication etc in England of the Wilson biography, do contact Jonathan Burnham, Chatto & Windus, 20 Vauxhall Bridge Rd, London SW1V 2SA.[1] Jonathan is now head of Chatto (England)—Carmen [Callil] having now taken over Australia and USA—and could be interested. I have mentioned etc.

Be well, don't be drowned, good you saw Rachel, with love & best wishes,

Iris

1   My *Edmund Wilson: A Biography* was published in London by Constable in 1995.

30 Charlbury Rd OX2 [September 4, 1993]

Dear Jeffrey,

Just to welcome you back to your home base! Thank you for your letter. What a powerful traveller you are! I wish I could visit that island off Bar Harbor, Maine! I'm sure I'd love the sea, I mean swimming in it, not just looking at it. I have had a few swims in the Thames, and only one in the sea this summer. I hardly ever see the stuff. Your mountain water place sounds good too.

DOI: 10.1057/9781137347909

Please excuse this hastily written note, we are just going away for a while. I am very tired. Will going away make me feel better or worse? Time will show. Much love, I

30 Charlbury Rd OX2 [September 27, 1993]

Dear Jeffrey,

Thank you for your splendid letter. You are wonderfully busy and you *get around* so very well. And you know modern literature and *modern writers* so much—you are splendid! I haven't seen Francis King's autobiography—I like him very much, though I now haven't seen him for some time.[1] Indeed I don't see many writers (tho' some are pals such as Andrew Wilson and A. S. Byatt).[2] I go on & on reading (just lately *War and Peace*—surely the greatest novel). What about *The Tale of Genji*? I love that. (By female, 1160 or so.)[3] I have finished a novel called *The Green Knight* (certain references to *Sir Gawain and*—)—I think you should receive a copy. If you *don't*, please let me know. It will be out in USA after Christmas, I believe. (It's just out here.) I endlessly envy your swimming! Much love, I

P.S. I *did* get some swimming actually, in Lake Como, but it rained all the time & was rather cold. I have also been to Ireland (Ulster), but I think I told you that before. Love.

1   Francis King, *Yesterday Came Suddenly* (1993), one of his best books.
2   A. S. (Antonia) Byatt (born 1936), English novelist and author of two books on Murdoch (1965 and 1976).
3   A classic Japanese novel, early eleventh century, by Lady Murasaki.

30 Charlbury Rd OX2 Nov 8 [1993]

Dearest Jeffrey,

So sorry not right [i.e., write]. I have a little been away (in bits and pieces), and have had to make speeches etc (I hate that) but mostly it is, as you say, the pile of papers. I receive more & more letters asking me to do things, all sorts of people, all sorts of things. Oh never mind, one should not complain, there are many lonely folk who are desperately waiting for attention.

The beautiful Oxford autumn is strewing the place with golden leaves. John is still tied up with St. Catherine's, D. Phil. students hang on to him,

DOI: 10.1057/9781137347909

and there are lots of other connections. He has just been (me with him) in Birmingham lecturing on A. E. Housman.

I see you are very busy as usual and *happy* with so many writings! Onward. I am trying (so far in vain) to start another novel. I hope a copy of my *Green Knight* reached you, if not *let me know*. I am really very tired & often forgetting things. I do wish I had an indoor swimming pool! Swimming (which you love I know) could relax me very much! Switching off the telephone is quite nice, except that one soon forgets one has done so. A secretary alas is impossible—I could not bear it! I daresay I shall *buck up* very soon.[1] The awful problems of [violence in] Ireland also distress me. Jeffrey dear, thank you so much for writing to me. With lots of love, I

1 Iris' headmistress at Badminton was always telling dispirited girls to "buck up."

30 Charlbury Road Oxford OX2 Nov 14 [1994]

My dear Jeffrey,

Thank you so much for your letter. I am so glad to have it! And what splendid news of Rachel, excellent girl, she will rise *very high*! And you are happy away from teaching. (So am I.) And now you are cornering Frost—onward, onward![1] *And* you met Malcolm B[radbury].[2] We haven't seen him for a long time. I have never tried Harbourfront. I am *sure* I *did* want to see you last summer (or *any* time!). I was partly away and partly very tired; and am now [in margin: less tired but] still not getting on with my present novel.[3] Hope better soon. I get so many requests from people who want me to *do* things. However we are having a wonderful exceptional autumn with golden brown leaves still on trees. I expect you are having one too.

I am *amazed* that someone has suggested that John and I are parted, divorced, this is absolutely *impossible*. We are utterly loving and forever together and well known to be, and have always been! Not an "oddity"— a perfect marriage—if that's odd! Please tell the crazy *someone* that it is a completely happy marriage, and he or she need not worry! I would be sorry if this false news "went around."

I hope you may be over here before too long, anyway in the summer, and do send messages thereof (and please reply to this letter, I hope). [in margin: no hurry, but do write.] N.B. you should *buy a house in France*!

Why not? Rachel will love it, and it will be *very useful* for her! *Sorry* for not writing sooner.

With much love,

Iris

1   Meyers, *Robert Frost: A Biography* (Boston: Houghton Mifflin, 1996).
2   Malcolm Bradbury (1932–2000), English novelist and professor, was the author of *Stepping Westward* (1968) and *The History Man* (1975).
3   Iris was an extremely fluent writer and always began her next novel immediately after finishing her previous one. Her difficulty with her last novel *Jackson's Dilemma* (1995) suggests, with hindsight, the first sign of the Alzheimer's disease that struck her three years later.

---

30 Charlbury Rd Oxford OX2 Nov 18 [1994]

P.S. Dearest Jeffrey,

Thank you very much indeed. EDMUND WILSON has just arrived! It's a great huge book, and we are already perusing it. You know so much—well done!—with love and thanks from Iris and John.

*There is so much about so many—a picture of America!

---

30 Charlbury Road Oxford OX2 [December 7, 1994]

Dearest Jeffrey,

Much thanks for your lively letter and the lovely POEM! It is indeed a *brilliant* poem and I feel it close to my heart.[1] What wonderful travels you have been on, how happy, and what a daughter. (I note French boyfriend, very good.) Here we haven't been on many journeys, except briefly to France. We haven't tried the Channel Tunnel yet. We are anyway enjoying the most warm and beautiful autumn since 1659! [i.e., 1959]. As I write the sky is pure blue (a few little white pretty clouds). I am wearing (often out) summer gear, and we wear light coats. [in margin: Not much rain.] However we are anxious about the *birds* and other such beings who seem to imagine it is spring.

We expect you will be over here in the summer (I hope it won't be rain and cold then.) Of course I am trying to write a novel, but it is unusually difficult. Signs of age and time perhaps. John was supposed to be

DOI: 10.1057/9781137347909

retired, but is constantly hauled back by St. Catherine's. He enjoys it on the whole. Oxford is so beautiful. Only trouble is 80 miles from the sea. *Thanks* for your lovely letter and poem!

All very best wishes & love from Iris

1   "White Flock" by the Russian poet Anna Akhmatova (1889–1966).

30 Charlbury Road Oxford OX2 [January 23, 1995]

Dear Jeffrey,

John has been having a splendid time with *Edmund Wilson*, and now I am at him. Many thanks! You write so beautifully and you *know* so much!

We have a rather crazy spring here, blue sky and birds singing.

Much love, I
You are really super.
[on envelope: We are into cats over here.]

[From John Bayley: On St. Catherine's College letterhead.] 30 Charlbury Rd [late 1997]

Dear Jeffrey,

I wish I could give you a more cheerful reply. Poor Iris is deep in Alzheimer's now. All scans & medication *etc* tried but nothing helps much, tho' she remains as *sweet* as ever. As you can imagine it's a 24 hour job, & the only time I get to do anything is the early morning sometimes; but it's very rewarding to look after Iris in a strange way, tho' nothing remains of her great creative mind, nothing.

So there we have it. Of course if you felt inclined to write something yourself, go ahead. I'm sometimes tempted to try a *sort* of personal memoir myself, if only as a distraction. Anyway, love to you both, & I do hope projects flourish. You are & have been a marvelously various biographer.

Best John

DOI: 10.1057/9781137347909

[From John Bayley. June 23, 1999]

Dear Jeffrey,

Thanks so much for letter & review. I do look forward to reading the memoir. Everything you write about Iris will be so welcome, & I am sorry Peter Conradi was rather off-putting—why shouldn't we all contribute our little piece to Iris studies!?[1] I have another one (this time with Norton—good publisher) due out autumn, but it's more about me really![2] My own memories & Iris's last year.... I shall look forward to whatever you write as always. Orwell will be good I'm sure.[3]

All best love to you both. John

1   When I asked John to identify some of my fellow lunch and dinner guests at Steeple Aston and Cornwall Gardens, Conradi replied: "John has asked me to say that, alas, he is not able to talk about Iris to anyone except her authorized biographer [Conradi]."
2   John published three memoirs: *Elegy for Iris* (1998), *Iris and Her Friends* (2000) and *Widower's House* (2001).
3   Meyers, *Orwell: Wintry Conscience of a Generation* (NY: Norton, 2000).

[From John Bayley. On St. Catherine's College letterhead. 2000.]

Dear Jeffrey,

So pleased you liked the Orwell review.[1] I liked the book *very* much, & *Privileged Moments* (excellent title!).[2] The Iris v. fine & Francis King & his mother & the Indian have entered Audi's & my personal mythology ("How am I knowing, Madam?").[3] A wonderfully perceptive & humorous book.

I have mixed feelings about the film, which I really didn't think would come off, but now it really looks like it may.[4] Judi Dench fine, but like *Shadowlands* it is bound to be a million miles from the reality of the thing.[5] Doesn't matter. I feel a bit rueful now that the contract, which I didn't look at properly (I had no agent then, never thought I needed one) took all film rights for the publisher! Well, it was the millionth chance that it would matter!

I look forward to your next. My wife Audi (one of Iris' & my oldest friends) is reading yr Orwell with great pleasure. XX to you both, John

1   John reviewed my *Orwell* in the *New York Review of Books*, 48 (March 29, 2001), 47–50.

DOI: 10.1057/9781137347909

2   Meyers, *Privileged Moments: Encounters with Writers* (Madison: University of Wisconsin Press, 2000).

3   When Francis King's aged mother tried to get the waiter in an Indian restaurant to flatter her about her youthful appearance, he overestimated her age by a decade. John had recently married the widow and old friend Audi Villers.

4   *Iris* (2001) starred Kate Winslet and Judi Dench as the young and older Iris, and Jim Broadbent as John.

5   *Shadowlands* (1993), a film about the Oxford don C. S. Lewis, starred Anthony Hopkins and Debra Winger.

DOI: 10.1057/9781137347909

A manuscript page from Murdoch's novel, The Message to the Planet

3
Interviews

Abstract: *The* Paris Review *interview describes Murdoch and Bayley's house in Oxford. Murdoch recalls her Irish family background and education, her wartime work in the civil service and with refugees in Europe; her politics. She describes her methods of composition, the creation of her characters; discusses her favorite novels, especially nineteenth century novels; philosophical and moral elements in novels; religious beliefs and Sartre; her plays; her enjoyment of paintings; her belief that novels need a good story. In the* Denver Quarterly *interview Murdoch describes her parents, schooling and time at Oxford in more detail; her war work and postwar experience in Europe; teaching at the Royal College of Art; her friendships.*

Meyers, Jeffrey. *Remembering Iris Murdoch: Letters and Interviews.* New York: Palgrave Macmillan, 2013.
DOI: 10.1057/9781137347909.

"The Art of Fiction CXVII: Iris Murdoch," *Paris Review*, 115 (Summer 1990), 206–225.

Iris Murdoch and her husband live in a house in academic north Oxford. In its comfortably untidy rooms books overflow the shelves and are piled high on the floor. Even the bathroom is filled with volumes on language, including Dutch and Esperanto grammar books. Her paper-strewn second-floor study is decorated with oriental rugs and with paintings of horses and children. The first floor sitting room, which leads out to the garden, has a well-stocked bar. There are paintings and tapestries of flowers, art books and records, pottery and old bottles, and embroidered cushions on the deep sofa.

INTERVIEWER

Do you think you could say something about your family?

IRIS MURDOCH

My father went through the first war in the cavalry; it now seems extraordinary to think there was cavalry in World War I. This no doubt saved his life, because, of course, the horses were behind the lines, and in that sense he had a safer war. My parents met at that time. My father's regiment was based at the Curragh near Dublin and my father was on leave. On his way to church he met my mother, who was going to the same church on the same tram. She sang in the choir. My mother had a very beautiful soprano voice; she was training to be an opera singer and could have been very good indeed, but she gave up her ambitions when she married. She continued singing all her life in an amateur way, but she never realized the potential of that great voice. She was a beautiful, lively, witty woman, with a happy temperament. My parents were very happy together. They loved each other dearly; they loved me and I loved them, so it was a most felicitous trinity.

INTERVIEWER

When did you know you wanted to write?

MURDOCH

I knew very early on that I wanted to be a writer. I mean, when I was a child I knew that. Obviously, the war disturbed all one's feelings of the future very profoundly. When I finished my undergraduate career I was immediately conscripted because everyone was. Under ordinary circumstances, I would very much have wanted to stay on at Oxford, study for a Ph.D., and try to become a don. I was very anxious to go on learning. But one had to sacrifice one's wishes to the war. I went into the civil

DOI: 10.1057/9781137347909

service, into the Treasury where I spent a couple of years. Then after the war I went into UNRRA, the United Nations Relief and Rehabilitation Association, and worked with refugees in different parts of Europe.

INTERVIEWER

You were a member of the Communist Party, weren't you?

MURDOCH

I was a member of the Communist Party for a short time when I was a student, about 1939. I went in, as a lot of people did, out of a sense which arose during the Spanish Civil War that Europe was dangerously divided between left and right and we were jolly well going to be on the left. We had passionate feelings about social justice. We believed that socialism could, and fairly rapidly, produce just and good societies, without poverty and without strife. I lost those optimistic illusions fairly soon. So I left it. But it was just as well, in a way, to have seen the inside of Marxism because then one realizes how strong and how awful it is, certainly in its organized form. My association with it had its repercussions. Once I was offered a scholarship to come to Vassar. I was longing to go to America— such an adventure after being cooped up in England after the war. One did want to travel and see the world. I was prevented by the McCarran Act, and not given a visa. I may say there was a certain amount of to-do about this. Bertrand Russell got involved and Justice Felix Frankfurter, trying to say how ridiculous this was. But the McCarran Act is made of iron. It's still here; I have to ask for a waiver if I want to come to the United States.

INTERVIEWER

Even now?

MURDOCH

It's lunatic. One of the questions sometimes asked by some official is, "Can you prove that you are no longer a member of the Communist Party?"

INTERVIEWER

I should think that would be very difficult to do.

MURDOCH

Extremely! I left it about fifty years ago!

INTERVIEWER

Could you tell me a little bit about your own method of composition and how you go about writing a novel?

DOI: 10.1057/9781137347909

MURDOCH

Well, I think it is important to make a detailed plan before you write the first sentence. Some people think one should write—"George woke up and knew that something terrible had happened yesterday"— and then see what happens. I plan the whole thing in detail before I begin. I have a general scheme and lots of notes. Every chapter is planned. Every conversation is planned. This is, of course, a primary stage, and very frightening because you've committed yourself at this point. I mean, a novel is a long job, and if you get it wrong at the start you're going to be very unhappy later on. The second stage is that one should sit quietly and let the thing invent itself. One piece of imagination leads to another. You think about a certain situation and then some quite extraordinary aspect of it suddenly appears. The deep things that the work is about declare themselves and connect. Somehow things fly together and generate other things, and characters invent other characters, as if they were all doing it themselves. One should be patient and extend this period as far as possible. Of course, actually writing it involves a different kind of imagination and work.

INTERVIEWER

You are remarkably prolific as a novelist. You seem to enjoy writing a great deal.

MURDOCH

Yes, I do enjoy it, but it has, of course—I mean, this is true of any art form—moments when you think it's awful, you lose confidence and it's all black. You can't think and so on. So, it's not all enjoyment. But I don't actually find writing in itself difficult. The *creation* of the story is the agonizing part. You have the extraordinary experience when you begin a novel that you are now in a state of unlimited freedom, and this is alarming. Every choice you make will exclude another choice, so that it's rather important what happens then, what state of mind you're in and what you think matters. Books should have themes. I choose titles carefully and the titles in some way indicate something deep in the theme of the book. Names are important. The names sometimes don't come at once, but the physical being and the mind of the character have to come pretty early on and you just have to wait for the gods to offer you something. You have to spend a lot of time looking out of the window and writing down scrappy notes which may or may not help. You have to wait patiently until you feel that you're getting the thing right—who the people are, what it's all about, how it moves. I may take a long time, say a year, just

DOI: 10.1057/9781137347909

sitting and fishing around, putting the thing into some sort of shape. Then I do a very detailed synopsis of every chapter, every conversation, everything that happens. That would be another operation.

INTERVIEWER

Which tends to come first—characters or plot?

MURDOCH

I think they all start in much the same way, with two or three people in a relationship with a problem. Then there is a story, ordeals, conflicts, a movement from illusion to reality, all that. I don't think I have any autobiographical tendencies and can't think of any novel I've written that is a copy of my own life.

INTERVIEWER

And you write by hand?

MURDOCH

Oh, yes, yes, yes.

INTERVIEWER

No machines, no computers?

MURDOCH

No.

INTERVIEWER

And then take them up to your publisher who's terrified because there's only one copy?

MURDOCH

Yes, at the end there's only one copy. I know that some people like word processors, but I do a great degree of correcting as I go along. I think if one had that green screen in front of one, one would be so fascinated by the words on it one wouldn't want to change any of them!

INTERVIEWER

What are your daily work habits?

MURDOCH

I like working and when I have time to work, I work. But I also have to do other things like washing up and buying food. Fortunately my husband does the cooking. I sometimes have to go to London or I want to see my friends. Otherwise, I work pretty steadily all the time. I go to bed early and I start work very early. I work all morning, and then I shop and write letters—the letters take up a lot of time—in the afternoon. Then

DOI: 10.1057/9781137347909

I work again from about half-past four until seven or eight. So I work steadily when I've got the open time, which is more days than not.

INTERVIEWER
How many words a day do you usually write?
MURDOCH
I've never thought of counting words. I'd rather not know.

INTERVIEWER
A moment ago you mentioned the names of your characters. How do you choose them?
MURDOCH
They have to choose themselves; one just waits. If you make a mistake there, this can be quite a serious matter. The character has to announce his own name. I make lists of names; I often invent names. I once invented the name Gavender; I thought, "Nobody's named Gavender." Then I got a letter from someone in America saying, "How did you know about our family?" It is fun inventing names. Names are very important because a lot of atmosphere comes with a name. The way a person is going to be addressed by his fellow characters is important, too.

INTERVIEWER
How do you find specific details about experts, like Bruno and his spiders, in your novels?
MURDOCH
I'm very interested in spiders. I like spiders. Spiders are my friends, and I have read books about spiders. So that part of the book was just part of a spider lore which I happen to possess.

INTERVIEWER
But if a man has a job like a wine merchant or soldier?
MURDOCH
I ask my wine merchant friends to help me. As for soldiers, my brother-in-law is a soldier. Everything to do with guns my husband, John, supplies because he is very interested in weapons. He knows all about weapons from the early Greeks to the latest machine guns. One's friends can help. And of course there are books.

INTERVIEWER
What's your most difficult technical problem?

DOI: 10.1057/9781137347909

MURDOCH

It's the one I mentioned earlier, the beginning, how to start and when to begin structuring the novel. It is this progression from complete freedom to a narrow cage, how fast you move and when you decide what the main things in the book are going to be. I think these are the most difficult things. One must consider what one's characters are like, what jobs they do, what religion they have, what nationality they are, how they are related to each other, and so on. Here at the beginning one has infinite possibilities, this choice of what sort of people they are and what sort of troubles they are going to have, who wins, who loses, who dies. Most of all one must reflect upon their values, their morality, their moral dilemmas. You can't write any novel without implying values. You can't write a traditional novel without giving your characters moral problems and judgments. That is what is most difficult of all.

INTERVIEWER

You've said that "one constantly takes prototypes from literature who may actually influence one's conduct." Could you give specific examples?

MURDOCH

Did I say that? Good heavens, I can't remember the context. Of course, one feels affection for, or identifies with, certain fictional characters. My two favorites are Achilles and Mr. Knightley. This shows the difficulty of thinking of characters who might influence one. I could reflect upon characters in Dickens, Dostoyevsky, Tolstoy; these writers particularly come to mind: wise moralistic writers who portray the complexity of morality and the difficulty of being good. Plato remarks in *The Republic* that bad characters are volatile and interesting, whereas good characters are dull and always the same. This certainly indicates a literary problem. It is difficult in life to be good, and difficult in art to portray goodness. Perhaps we don't know much about goodness. Attractive bad characters in fiction may corrupt people, who think, "So that's okay." Inspiration from good characters may be rarer and harder, yet Alyosha in *The Brothers Karamazov* and the grandmother in Proust's novel exist. I think one is influenced by the whole moral atmosphere of literary works, just as we are influenced by Shakespeare, a great exemplar for the novelist. In the most effortless manner he portrays moral dilemmas, good and evil, and the differences and the struggle between them. I think he is a deeply religious writer. He doesn't portray religion directly in the plays, but it is certainly there, a sense of the spiritual, of

DOI: 10.1057/9781137347909

goodness, of self-sacrifice, of reconciliation and of forgiveness. I think that is the absolutely prime example of how we ought to tell a story: invent characters and convey something dramatic which at the same time has deep spiritual significance.

INTERVIEWER

If your fictional characters are not based on real people, as they are for most novelists, for example Hemingway and Lawrence, then how are your characters created?

MURDOCH

Just by this process of sitting and waiting. I would abominate the idea of putting real people into a novel, not only because I think it's morally questionable, but also because I think it would be terribly dull. I don't want to make a photographic copy of somebody I know. I want to create somebody who never existed, and who is at the same time a plausible person. I think the characteristics gradually gather together. The first image of the character may be very shadowy; one vaguely knows that he is a good citizen or a religious sort of chap. Perhaps he's puritanical, or hedonistic, and so on. I must have some notion of the troubles he's going to be in and his relationship to the other characters. But the details on which the novel depends, the details of his appearance, his peculiarities, his idiosyncrasies, his other characteristics, his mode of being, will come later—if one is lucky—and quite instinctively, because the more you see of a person the more a kind of coherence begins to evolve.

INTERVIEWER

Your characters are not necessarily innocents. They're able to commit violence and all sorts of misdeeds, and yet there exists this imperative within them toward the good. Does philosophy apply here?

MURDOCH

I don't think this connects with philosophy. The consideration of moral issues in the novels may be intensified by some philosophical considerations, but on the whole I think it's dangerous writing a philosophical novel. I mean, this is not a thing writers can easily get away with. Take the case of Thomas Mann, whom I adore, for instance. When his characters start having very long philosophical conversations, one feels, "Well, perhaps we could do without this." My novels are not "philosophical novels."

DOI: 10.1057/9781137347909

INTERVIEWER

Well, your characters also have long philosophical arguments.

MURDOCH

Well, occasionally, but not very long.

INTERVIEWER

You once wrote, "A great artist is, in respect of his work, a good man and in the true sense a free man." I wonder if you could interpret that?

MURDOCH

The important phrase is, "…in respect to his work," because obviously great artists can lead less than perfect lives. Take Dante for instance. Or Shakespeare. We know very little about Shakespeare's life. You could name almost anybody who has written a great or good novel and see that their lives are imperfect. You can be unselfish and truthful in your art, and a monster at home. To write a good book you have to have certain qualities. Great art is connected with courage and truthfulness. There is a conception of truth, a lack of illusion, an ability to overcome selfish obsessions, which goes with good art, and the artist has got to have that particular sort of moral stamina. Good art, whatever its style, has qualities of hardness, firmness, realism, clarity, detachment, justice, truth. It is the work of a free, unfettered, uncorrupted imagination. Whereas bad art is the soft, messy self-indulgent work of an enslaved fantasy. Pornography is at one end of that scale, great art at the other end.

The reading of great books, the contemplation of great art, is somehow very good for one. There's a truthfulness of great art which one sees in the great nineteenth-century novels. It is very difficult to attain, to create something which is not a fantasy. I'd want to make a distinction between fantasy and imagination, not the same as Coleridge's, but a distinction between the expression of immediate selfish feelings and the elimination of yourself in a work of art. The most obvious case of the former would be the novel where the writer is the hero and is always succeeding. He doesn't succeed at first, but he's very brave, and all the girls like him, and so on. That tends to spoil the work. I think some of D. H. Lawrence's work is spoiled by too much Lawrence. What is important is an ability to have an image of perfection and to expel fantasy and the sort of lesser, egoistic cravings and the kind of imagery and immediate expressions that might go with them, and to be prepared to think and to wait. It's difficult, as I say, to make this into any sort of program, to overcome egoism and fantasy.

DOI: 10.1057/9781137347909

INTERVIEWER

What would be an example in the novel?

MURDOCH

There would be very obvious cases—the whole tradition of the English novel from Jane Austen, Charles Dickens, Emily Brontë, George Eliot and, of course, Henry James, whom I love. I also love the Russian novel. In a curious way English-speaking people feel a great affinity with the Russians. Somehow, the works of Tolstoy and Dostoyevsky in translation seem very natural to us. It's as if they were already writing in English. I think that we have the same feeling about Proust—that he's really an English writer! He speaks to us very directly…whereas Stendhal and Flaubert are more remote. We know they're French. It was the great age of the novel. One can always return to them and find marvelous wisdom.

INTERVIEWER

Should the novelist also be a moralist and teacher?

MURDOCH

Moralist, yes. Teacher suggests something rather more didactic in tone. A novelist is bound to express values, and I think he should be conscious of the fact that he is, in a sense, a compulsory moralist. Novelists differ, of course, in the extent to which they set out to reflect on morals and to put that reflection into their work. I certainly do reflect and put this reflection into my works, whether or not with success. The question is how to do it. If you can't do it well, you had better not do it at all. If you have strong moral feelings, you may be in difficulties with your characters because you may want them to be less emphatic than you are yourself. In answer to your question, I think a novelist should be wary of being a teacher in a didactic sense, but should be conscious of himself as a moralist.

INTERVIEWER

In your work you consider what religion means for people who do not believe in God. Can you say something about this?

MURDOCH

This question interests and concerns me very much. Looking at western societies I think that if we have religion, we shall have to have religion without God, because belief in a personal God is becoming increasingly impossible for many people. It's a difficult question actually to know what believing in a personal God is. I know that I don't believe in one. I don't want to use the word "God" in any other sense. I

DOI: 10.1057/9781137347909

think it's a proper name. I don't believe in the divinity of Christ. I don't believe in life after death. My beliefs really are Buddhist in style. I've been very attached to Buddhism. Buddhism makes it plain that you can have religion without God, that religion is in fact better off without God. It has to do with *now*, with every moment of one's life, how one thinks, what one is and does, about love and compassion and the overcoming of self, the difference between illusion and reality.

INTERVIEWER

In your book on Jean-Paul Sartre, you write of a kind of breakdown of moral authority, the disappearance of religion and a sense of chaos that's ushered in and reflects itself in your work.

MURDOCH

Well, it's a long way back to the Sartre era. His popularity immediately after the war was extraordinary. People who had nothing to do with philosophy felt that a philosophy had been invented for them. The war had been so terrible and so destructive, and the Hitler era had been so unimaginably awful. People wanted to find a way of having some kind of spirit come back into their life. Sartre's existentialist ethic with its notion of complete freedom, and the notion that you should get yourself into a state where you can make a choice which transcends conventions and the dull feeling of being contained, submerged, and so on—this (and his novels, too) reflects, in a way, a heroic ethic. It did cheer people up a lot. I don't particularly go along with this myself, but it had a great revivifying effect.

INTERVIEWER

I wondered how you feel about your own achievements and what you've done?

MURDOCH

Well, one is always discontented with what one has done. And also, of course, one's always afraid that even the things one has done can't be done again. I don't know. I think artists live in the present, really. I mean, forget about the past and what you've done because it's what you think you can do *next* which matters. For any writer it's terribly discouraging if somebody says, "Oh, I loved your first novel!" My heart sinks when they say that, because that suggests it's been downhill all the way!

DOI: 10.1057/9781137347909

INTERVIEWER

What were you able to accomplish in the play, *The Black Prince,* that you did not accomplish in the novel?

MURDOCH

Well, the theater is such a different game. Writers of fiction, of novels, are pleased when they can see something of their work on the stage and hear people uttering their lines and so on. But a play is made of lines, and it's got to be…I mean, the miracle about the theater is why people stay there. Why don't they get up and go? It's not at all easy to write a play. There's a special kind of magic involved. My first adventure in the theater was a very pleasant one because I worked with J. B. Priestley on making a play out of a novel of mine called *A Severed Head.* He said to me, "Duckie, this is a difficult game; a very few people can succeed at it. If it was all that easy everybody would be doing it." It is very difficult to compress the reflections of one's characters and the great pattern of a novel into drama where it is a matter of lines and short speeches and actual actors and so on. The forms are so different that they can't possibly be compared. A play is much more like a poem.

INTERVIEWER

Could you say something about your use of painters and painting in fiction? I'm thinking of Max Beckmann in *Henry and Cato,* Bronzino in *The Nice and the Good,* Titian in *The Sacred and Profane Love Machine.*

MURDOCH

I am very interested in painting. Painting appears more frequently than music, for instance, because I know far more about painting than about music. The only music which tends to appear is singing, which I know about because of my mother. I love painting. I love looking at pictures, and I did once very much want to be a painter. I understand painting in a way I don't understand music, though I am moved by music. I know a lot of painters. I know what painting is. I enjoy bringing in painting. I loved doing the Beckmann business in *Henry and Cato.* I admire Beckmann very much and I've seen a lot of Beckmanns in St. Louis and other places. With a bit of luck, one's own interests and feelings can run straight along with those of the character. But there is also the challenge of inventing characters with alien interests. This can be a dangerous business.

DOI: 10.1057/9781137347909

INTERVIEWER

Do you see a painting you are particularly interested in and think, "I might be able to use that some day in a novel," or "I'd like to use it because it attracts and interests me"?

MURDOCH

The novel often indicates a painting during the process of creating the characters. Somehow the character will lead to the painting. A great painting which I have only recently seen—it lives in Czechoslovakia—is Titian's *Flaying of Marsyas*. He was over ninety when he painted it. This painting gives me very much, though I have only referred to it indirectly.

INTERVIEWER

Does your husband read and comment on your works before they're published?

MURDOCH

No, he doesn't see them until they're printed. I talk to him occasionally about things where he can help me, about how a revolver works or something like that.

INTERVIEWER

Do you show parts of the novel to your editor at Chatto & Windus before it's completed?

MURDOCH

No, I don't show it to them until I've finished it. I don't ask for advice.

INTERVIEWER

Do you think children limit the freedom needed as a writer?

MURDOCH

Oh, no. There are innumerable examples of their compatibility. Women have obvious problems about family life and doing jobs. But, in a way, being a writer is one of the easier choices because you can do it at home. I don't think there is an awful problem there.

INTERVIEWER

Which contemporary writers do you respect?

MURDOCH

I don't really read contemporary writers very much. For instance, I enjoyed reading Kundera's *The Unbearable Lightness of Being,* Ishiguro's *A Pale View of Hills,* and A.S. Byatt's wonderful novel, *Possession.*

DOI: 10.1057/9781137347909

INTERVIEWER

Do you read the works of writers you know?

MURDOCH

Yes, sometimes. But I don't read much contemporary fiction. I particularly admire John Cowper Powys. I particularly like *Wolf Solent, A Glastonbury Romance* and *Weymouth Sands*. They are very long novels, full of details which novels should have. I think he is very good on sex. Sex is a complicated, subtle, omnipresent, mysterious, multifarious business; sex is everywhere. I think Hardy is a far more erotic writer than Lawrence. John Cowper Powys is really interested in sex, just as keen on it as Lawrence, but he understands and portrays it far better. He sees so many different aspects of it. He treats it with reverence and respect. He finds it very strange, and funny, and mysterious.

INTERVIEWER

What effect would you like your books to have?

MURDOCH

I'd like people to enjoy reading them. A readable novel is a gift to humanity. It provides an innocent occupation. Any novel takes people away from their troubles and the television set; it may even stir them to reflect about human life, characters, morals. So I would like people to be able to read the stuff. I'd like it to be understood too; though some of the novels are not all that easy, I'd like them to be understood, and not grossly misunderstood. But literature is to be enjoyed, to be grasped by enjoyment.

INTERVIEWER

How would you describe your ideal reader?

MURDOCH

Those who like a jolly good yarn are welcome and worthy readers. I suppose the *ideal* reader is someone who likes a jolly good yarn and enjoys thinking about the book as well, thinking about the moral issues.

INTERVIEWER

Do you think a good yarn is essential to the novel?

MURDOCH

It is one of the main charms of the art form and its prime mode of exposition. A novel without a story must work very hard in other ways to be worth reading, and indeed to be read. Some of today's anti-story novels are too deliberately arcane. I think story is essential to the survival of the novel. A novel may be "difficult" but its story can carry and

DOI: 10.1057/9781137347909

retain the reader who may understand in his own way, even remember
and return. Stories are a fundamental human form of thought.

"An Interview with Iris Murdoch," *Denver Quarterly*, 26 (Summer 1991), 102–111.

MEYERS

Could you describe your parents?

MURDOCH

I had wonderful parents. I'm an only child and I enjoyed the comfort
and inspiration of these delightful people over a very long period. My
father died much earlier than my mother, who died only recently. It
dawned on me much later that it's not all that usual for people to have
perfect relations with their parents. I certainly did enjoy that.

My mother's family (whose name is Richardson) were landed gentry.
By the time I arrived on the scene their fortunes had changed. They
didn't possess the estates any more; they were living in Dublin, and were
mostly lawyers and soldiers. My father came from a family of yeoman
farmers in County Down and from the name I imagine that my remoter
ancestors came from Galloway, in Scotland. In fact, my mother's family
and my father's family probably arrived in Ireland around the same time,
which would have been the early seventeenth century, when a lot of Scots
farmers were settled there. Through an odd fluke my father was born in
New Zealand. His part of the family set off to be farmers in that country,
and then came back rather abruptly to County Down, just after he was
born, possibly because my grandfather inherited land there.

My father decided, as I see it now it was a bold decision, to leave
Ireland with my mother and me immediately after the Great War and
seek his fortune in England. He entered the civil service at some modest level and worked his way to the top. He was a very clever man but
without ambition. He probably used up a lot of energy getting himself
out of Ireland and establishing himself in England. He didn't want to be
very powerful. He enjoyed being a civil servant.

He was in the Ministry of Health most of his life, later in the General
Registrar Office. He was a very literary man, he loved books and tales. I
could read at an early age, he wanted to discuss books with me, so I was
reading *Treasure Island*, *Kim* and the Alice stories. These were the first
books that I remember enjoying, and I discussed them with my father.

DOI: 10.1057/9781137347909

We were always reading novels or discussing them with each other and this was a great source of pleasure to us both.

MEYERS

How did your parents influence you?

MURDOCH

I think my father was a really good man; I didn't realize how remarkable this was until later on. He was a great inspiration to me and certainly the greatest influence in my life. He wasn't a religious man in any ordinary sense. I was brought up as an Anglican, I went to church when I was at school, I also went to Quaker meetings. My parents occasionally went to church, but they weren't regular attenders, following the tradition of my mother's family, who were cheerful, relaxed Anglicans. My father had exceptional integrity, truthfulness and compassion. He had very high moral standards, though not in a priggish sense. He had a certain simplicity, was humorous and romantic.

MEYERS

Did any teachers at Badminton School influence you significantly?

MURDOCH

The headmistress of my school influenced me. Many of the people at the school were Quakers, and she too was a member of the Society of Friends. I went to this eccentric and, I think, very good school. It was rather left-wing (it's unusual to find a left-wing girls' boarding school), with enlightened liberal views and an internationally-minded idealistic ethos. We were to serve the world and help our society, and also seek academic excellence. We were interested in politics and world affairs, world peace and the League of Nations. This was before the second war.

Everything was taught at that school—Greek and Latin, mathematics, chemistry, pottery, cricket, music; whatever was going, we learned it. I was terribly homesick to begin with because of being parted from my parents, but I think it was a good experience. Indira Gandhi was there as my contemporary, and I knew her and kept in touch with her throughout her life. A lot of left-wing people, such as the Gollancz family, sent their children to that school. It was a "progressive school" in the best sense, combining orderly discipline with government by consent. We worked hard and expressed our thoughts freely. The headmistress, Miss Baker, was a remarkable woman, a dominating person, an old-fashioned

DOI: 10.1057/9781137347909

idealistic socialist and a great preacher of the liberation of women, who believed that education was education in virtue.

MEYERS

Who influenced you in Oxford?

MURDOCH

One of the things that impressed me when I came to Oxford was the sense of an enormously high standard. It was like seeing Mount Everest, meeting with the great scholars, and having the gratifying feeling that they actually knew you existed and were prepared to talk to you. There are many people I could mention, but perhaps two are Eduard Fraenkel, professor of Latin, and the historian Arnaldo Momigliano. Both these great men, who were always my teachers, were later my friends. They belonged to a tradition (now alas fading) that expected scholars to know several languages and also all history and all literature.

MEYERS

Why did you briefly join the Communist Party as a student?

MURDOCH

I did go through this time of being a Marxist and reading a great deal of Marx and Marxist writings. I think it was a good thing to have seen the inside of Marxism, and to have learned there Marxist things which ought to be learned, but which are now taken for granted. With Marx as with Freud, there are many true things which they believed and which have come to be accepted. I also learned, inside the Party, how terrible this organization is, or was. I am glad to have lived to see its destruction. The Party provides a frightening example of how a small number of opinionated, ruthless people can disrupt a society, as in Lebanon or Northern Ireland.

MEYERS

How did you happen to get a job, just after university, in the wartime Treasury?

MURDOCH

Like everyone else, I was conscripted. I could have gone into the women's forces, school-teaching, the land army, a factory or some sort of civil administration. One couldn't just sit around and arrange the flowers or pursue academic studies. Ten days after I'd finished my exams I was in Whitehall. My father was a civil servant and he was keen that I should be a career civil servant, which I didn't particularly want to be. (Of course

DOI: 10.1057/9781137347909

he also wanted me to be a novelist.) As it was, I didn't like the other options open to me and I wasn't allowed to go on studying, so I decided to try for the civil service. I was allotted to the Treasury, which is the top department, and my father was delighted. I was in the department which was concerned with the internal arrangements of the civil service, with elaborations of the pay structures in relation to the war, not perhaps thrilling stuff in itself, but complex and various, and I enjoyed doing it. I gained the utmost respect for the civil service at that time. I found it full of very intelligent, well-intentioned and hard-working people. I was thrown in the deep end—I was in the administrative class, an Assistant Principal—and was expected to be able to master the stuff pretty quickly. I found this most invigorating. We had two weeks' holiday in the year and worked five-and-a-half days a week. It was certainly a change from Oxford; it was also pretty enlivening to be in the middle of London during the war, particularly in the second part of the Blitz when V1s and V2s were landing. Of course it was frightening, but it was a time I wouldn't have missed.

MEYERS

How did your postwar refugee work affect your fiction?

MURDOCH

I don't think it affected it very much, except for a strong feeling about refugees. I've never attempted to portray anything that happened to me either during the war or afterward in the refugee camps. I don't think I have an impulse to use my life in that way. The interest in refugees probably started at school. At this enlightened place we had a lot of scholarships for Jewish girls so we knew about refugees before the war. All these clever girls were arriving. We knew about Hitler. So the concept of the refugee came to me very early, together with the concept of being Jewish. After the war, I worked in the UNRRA camps for displaced persons who were victims of Hitler, such as people who had been working as forced labor in factories: Poles, Czechs and Yugoslavs, all sorts of people who were lost and destitute. Some sort of feeling about homelessness and exile came out of that experience.

MEYERS

Do you have any contact in England with the refugees you worked with in Europe?

DOI: 10.1057/9781137347909

MURDOCH

Only two or three. Most of these people didn't want to go back to their homeland. They'd had enough of Europe and wanted to go to America, and some of the younger ones did. The older ones, of course, just got left in the camps. Nobody wanted them and God knows what happened to them. One was very much concerned with helping people to go where they wanted to go and some of these refugees wanted to go to England. In fact, there were several cases where I managed to help people who wanted to come over here. But the most successful long-standing contact was a Yugoslav.

I was working in Graz, in Austria—I worked in several different camps in several parts of Austria—and Graz University set up a camp for students. They had refugees who were studying and the university gave them facilities. This young Yugoslav chap was a medical student, and when we first met our common language was German, which we both spoke badly but with great mutual comprehension. He wanted to come to England and I did help him to get into medical school. Now he is a head consultant in Bristol and has had a very successful career. But he was one of the lucky ones.

MEYERS

After the war you taught philosophy at Oxford and began to write novels. Why did you begin to teach at the Royal College of Art in the mid-1960s?

MURDOCH

That was really for fun. I decided that I would give up teaching at Oxford, which was a hard decision; I didn't want to, but I couldn't go on doing quite so many things at once. So I gave that up. At the same time a friend of mine who was running the General Studies department at the Royal College said, "we're looking for someone to teach some philosophy to our students," so I thought, "why shouldn't I?" It was a day-a-week job. I am very interested in painting, I really wanted to be a painter at one time, and it was a very nice job to teach these kids. Many of them were painters and sculptors, and very intelligent, but had never read a book. It was a challenging, exciting operation talking to these lively young people who were much wilder than Oxford students and very picturesque. It gave me insight into the art school world and I was interested in seeing painters and sculptors at work.

DOI: 10.1057/9781137347909

MEYERS

What were the effects of your move from Steeple Aston, a country village, to Oxford?

MURDOCH

Convenience, shopping, no long car journeys. I miss the big garden and the lovely house, but it was getting too difficult to cope with. It's a more convenient life here. I see more of my Oxford friends.

MEYERS

Who are your closest literary friends and what have you learned from them?

MURDOCH

I don't think I learn anything literary from them, but I may learn a lot of other things. Kingsley Amis is an old friend, I've known him since we were students. Also, for instance, A. S. Byatt, A. N. Wilson, Andrew Harvey, Bernice Rubens, Vikram Seth. I think I have more friends who are scholars or painters or do other things.

MEYERS

How do you use your travels in your work?

MURDOCH

Not much, really. One of my novels, *Nuns and Soldiers,* has a scene in a French landscape, the Alpines, north of Marseilles, but that is a landscape that I know very well and have a strong feeling about.

MEYERS

What are the benefits of attending international cultural conferences?

MURDOCH

Fun, travel, friends, occasionally thoughts. I met Vikram Seth at a conference in Delhi. One sometimes meets someone one really wants to know, and one meets one's old friends. One may even, actually, get some ideas out of the discussion. It can be valuable. Yes, I think that one gets a lot out of traveling to another place, meeting a lot of intellectuals and just collecting one's wits, thinking of something to say and thinking about what people think about what you have to say. I think there is some value in this. I feel very strongly about Europe, that it's important for Europeans to get used to being in one another's pockets. I feel this very much about France and England, that we should be closer than we are.

DOI: 10.1057/9781137347909

MEYERS

Could you tell me specifically how any one of your novels was conceived? What idea, plot or characters you started with, and how you planned the book before writing?

MURDOCH

The Book and the Brotherhood obviously came out of an interest in Marxism and the way in which people's ideas changed, out of having a lot of friends at the university. It concerned the way in which differences of opinion define people; the notion of a book which at one time everyone felt was going to express their views and later on realized it wasn't. So it's got some sort of connection with Oxford and Marxism.

MEYERS

Did you have any breakthrough or crucial turning point in the course of your career that, looking back, seems to be particularly important?

MURDOCH

There is a progression from *Under the Net* to *The Bell*. *Under the Net* was a sort of freak novel, and *The Bell* was the beginning of a more traditional mode of proceeding. I think my later books are better than my earlier books. Of course every writer wants to think this, nobody wants to think it's all been downhill! I think the later books are better, and I think they started getting better round about the stage of *The Nice and the Good* and *A Word Child*.

MEYERS

What is the function and meaning of the homosexual characters who appear quite frequently in your novels?

MURDOCH

I think it depends on the context. They play different parts in different stories. I know a lot of homosexuals. I have homosexual friends. I'm very much in favor of gay lib, and I feel very strongly that there shouldn't be any sort of prejudice against homosexuals, or suggestions that homosexual love is unnatural or bad. I hope such views are tending to disappear from society.

MEYERS

How are your political beliefs, about Ireland, for example, expressed in your fiction?

DOI: 10.1057/9781137347909

MURDOCH

My book about Ireland, *The Red and the Green*, was written before the IRA started up again, so that it was, as it were, an innocent, optimistic book which assumed the troubles were over. I was born in Dublin, but moved to London when I was about one. But I've very often been in Ireland and I have relations in both Dublin and Belfast. I have a strong sense of being Irish. When people say to me, "oh, I see you're Anglo-Irish, not really Irish," this enrages me. I am completely Irish, my ancestors lived there for centuries. But now, of course, one's heart is broken over Ireland. I don't think we can go on talking about this because I have such strong emotions about it. The activity of the IRA exhibits the extreme of human wickedness. It is an example of how a few evil people can maim a whole society. It is a tragic situation, often misunderstood by people in other countries.

MEYERS

You have been described as an idealist without illusions. Would you agree with this?

MURDOCH

I'm an idealist, I suppose, yes. Whether one is without illusions is difficult to say. I should think I probably have illusions. I think there are a lot of half-illusions which one has where one is half-deceived or half-deceiving oneself. Being an idealist suggests that one has certain hopes, and I have lots and lots of hopes, and, I suppose, ideals. I feel very optimistic in one way and very pessimistic in other ways, and this may sometimes be difficult to adjust. One hopes that one is going to be able to partake in or witness some good change in the world or in oneself. Then someone comes along and says, "you're not looking at the facts, you're not being realistic, it can't happen like this, you just think it would be nice if it did." But hope and optimism can be justified. Consider the recent changes in eastern Europe. Hope is said to be a virtue, a kind of attention which may illuminate the way to the good.

MEYERS

In your work, you consider what religion is for people without God. Could you say more about this?

MURDOCH

Traditional religions, Judaism and Christianity, have given us contexts in which to think about love and compassion and the overcoming of self, the difference between illusion and reality. Both Hinduism and

DOI: 10.1057/9781137347909

Buddhism too, in different ways, offer a tremendous structure which I see no reason to jettison. So one is really wanting to keep the structure and the stories, but to live religion without the problems which a lot of people worry about—whether the old literal beliefs are true or not. I think the old literal beliefs are picturesque. I can't make any sense of the idea of another life or another place or of a person called God. I grew up in Anglican Christianity and I feel in a way I'm still inside the Anglican church. Some Anglican clerics come very near to saying this sort of thing. But I think this sort of thing should be said more. People should realize that when you lose the literalistic beliefs of your religion you are not losing religion, that religion is a deeper matter. It is not the same as lofty morality. Matthew Arnold said that religion was just morality plus emotion, and this seems to me to be an entire misunderstanding of the human situation. I thought of becoming a Buddhist, but I'm really a Christian Buddhist. I see no reason to lose my Christianity. Whether Christianity can survive and "demythologize" itself, to use that horrible modern term, in time to go on appealing to people and being significant, I don't know. I think it's one of the most important problems on the planet—what's going to happen to religion.

MEYERS

What do you hope to achieve in your future work?

MURDOCH

To write better novels. Also, perhaps, to write some decent philosophy. Maybe to write something more for the theater. One of my plays, *The Servants and the Snow* (performed by the Greenwich Theatre) was made into a splendid opera (with my libretto) by William Mathias, and performed by the Welsh National Opera. Another play called *The Three Arrows*, set in medieval Japan, was performed by the Actors Company, with Ian McKellen as hero. I think it could also make a good musical. A play by me based on *The Black Prince* ran for a while at the Aldwych Theatre in London, with Ian McDiarmid as Bradley Pearson.

MEYERS

Do you think your books have been generally understood?

MURDOCH

I don't know. I get letters which I value from people who say that my books have helped them in some way. That's pleasing news.

DOI: 10.1057/9781137347909

Passages Deleted by Iris from our *Paris Review* interview

The work of civil servants:

"[My father] did what civil servants do. They organise legislation, they clarify the whole background of the organisation of society. They are not supposed to be directly involved in politics, but political issues of course cross their paths. And they make moral judgements. It's hard to say exactly what they do because in different departments the subject matter is very different. Now there is a new minister of health, who must consider the whole problem of the relation of parliamentary legislation to the institutions which affect it. Civil servants are concerned with these transitions."

Illusions about Socialism:

"[We had] understandable illusions about what Socialism was and how we were going to bring about Socialism. We didn't have any clear idea about how we were going to do this. We thought that Capitalism was preventing justice in society and Socialism was going to produce it. Well, these were illusions which I lost fairly rapidly."

Experiencing the London Blitz:

"Although it was certainly frightening, it sort of stirred the spirit. It was certainly a remarkable scene. In fact, one might very well have perished at that time. The windows of the flat I lived in were blown in on more than one occasion. Everyone's windows were blown in by a blast and one had to find somebody to put up some wooden windows instead. Then the wooden windows would be blown in, and so on. I mean there was plenty going on in the middle of London at that time. I think I learned a lot just from seeing these high-powered bureaucrats at work, seeing how they worked and learning respect for them."

Move from Steeple Aston to Oxford:

"One could have spent all one's time simply looking after things in the garden. It meant also that I had to plan my day. Either I was going to be in Oxford or I was going to be in Steeple Aston. Dodging to and fro wasn't particularly easy because of the distance. It still gives me gratification to think I can go out and shop and buy a lot of different things. We

DOI: 10.1057/9781137347909

had a tiny village shop but even that packed up after a while. So that it's just the comforts of civilisation and a warm house, which we never had before."

Characters in nineteenth-century novels:

"Of course the novelists of today are not to be compared with the great novelists of the nineteenth and early twentieth century, who were geniuses upon whom we meditate, and who can teach us about morality and about how human lives are to be lived. And I think that one's love for certain characters, though one loves all sorts of bad as well as good characters, can be difficult. I can think of novels that have influenced me, but not exactly as a writer."

IRA:

"It's so terrible what's happened to that island. I mean particularly the IRA, but also Protestant terrorists who eventually, after some time, started up in imitation of the IRA. And there is also the demoralization of the children. I'm thinking of Ulster and of the children who grow up in an atmosphere of hatred and fear. And of the number of wicked actions, continuous murders which sow problems for years and years ahead. How will they get out of this condition of hatred and acceptance of continually murderous activity? I don't know. I think terrorism is a great problem for civilized societies. It blots my feelings about Ireland very much. I just feel grief and stress about it."

D. H. Lawrence:

"I think Lawrence's didactic views about sex chill the blood. To hold a kind of narrow dogma about it the way he did is, I think, very discouraging. People don't necessarily feel that Lawrence's sort of idealisation of sex is the way in which sex enters their lives."

Whether a good book must be produced by a good character:

"I don't think good books are always made by good characters. Plato said it's easy to create a bad character and difficult to create a good character. So the implication would be that if there are successful good characters, some greater ability than normal has been shown by the writer. It's easy

DOI: 10.1057/9781137347909

enough to write about romantic, selfish persons and much more difficult to write about romantic good persons.

I think there is a kind of virtue which a good artist must possess. So there is something in the idea that a good book is written by a good person. But it's a narrow sense of good. It would be that he's a virtuous, patient, truthful artist, who can govern his imagination in a certain way and take it away from egoism. But if you start looking at the lives of individuals, you very often see the virtue in their art is not in their life, except in relation to their art."

Understanding her novels:

"Some of my novels are not that easy to understand, that is, they involve problems about religion and morality and, of course, references to intellectual matters which might make them difficult. But I would obviously like everyone to enjoy reading them."

Negative letters about her books:

"Of course, I don't know people who were damaged by them or didn't like them, and wouldn't write letters to me."

Ideal readers and the survival of the novel:

"Some of the deliberately arcane and fearful books, which people sometimes feel compelled to write now, are difficult to understand. Obviously, a great traditional novel can be difficult to understand too, but one wants the novel form to survive. I think great novels won't survive if people don't feel it's a jolly nice thing to read a story."

DOI: 10.1057/9781137347909

4

On the Memoirs of A. N. Wilson and John Bayley

Abstract: *This chapter discusses the memoirs of Murdoch published after her death. The amusing and incisive* Iris Murdoch As I Knew Her *by A. N. Wilson describes her complex and contradictory character in detail. John Bayley's tender* Elegy for Iris *records how he cared for her in her last years, and how he finally possessed the often promiscuous and elusive Iris.*

Meyers, Jeffrey. *Remembering Iris Murdoch: Letters and Interviews*. New York: Palgrave Macmillan, 2013. DOI: 10.1057/9781137347909.

I

A. N. Wilson, the English historian, biographer and novelist, was an Oxford student and friend of Iris and John for thirty years. He was also, at one time, her authorized biographer. His amusing and incisive memoir, *Iris Murdoch As I Knew Her* (2003), has a good deal to say about her novels, includes her brief biography and explains why he never wrote the big book. More perceptive than Peter Conradi, who's mainly content to collect the facts, Wilson abundantly provides the malice missing from Iris' letters. Angry about the enthusiastic praise of John Bayley's *Elegy for Iris*, he unleashes a sharp attack on John's character and book.

Referring to Iris by her initials, Wilson states: "This book is an attempt to get hold of IM, to prise out her secret.... I have been trying to match my own encounters with her, and the things which she said to me over the years, with the success and failures of her fictions." He says that knowing Iris was an incalculable privilege, and describes her as secretive and mysterious, a mixture of spirituality and sensuality, with strangely skewed values: "incest perfectly OK. Cheating in exams unthinkable." He writes that her seductive "voice was deep, musical, [a] mixture of old Oxford and Northern Ireland.... It sounds like the voice of Wisdom itself: it is playful, but serious."

Unlike most commentators, Wilson also notes her negative qualities. Though novelists are not obliged to tell the truth, he's surprised that she guarded her privacy "by shameless and habitual social lying" about her background and personal life. Though well aware of her own worth, she was jealous of contemporary rivals like Olivia Manning, Elizabeth Taylor and Jean Rhys, and "found praise of Muriel Spark hard to stomach." Passionate about Irish politics, "she identified entirely with the Protestants of the North, and regarded the [fanatical leader] Reverend Ian Paisley with indulgent affection." Wilson wittily compares his friendship with Iris to the relations of "Julie Andrews and the Abbess in *The Sound of Music*." And he wonders (as I did), since Iris was prepared to go to bed with anyone, whether he himself might have had a brief fling with her.

Wilson carefully examines the vexed question of Iris' childless marriage. He correctly states that John "'hated kids' and persuaded himself that IM had never wanted them." But when Wilson asked why she'd never had children, Iris wept and regretfully said, "that was something which was not to be"—either because they couldn't conceive a child or John

DOI: 10.1057/9781137347909

refused to have one. She once told Wilson that "she would very much have liked to have children and she envied those who had done so."

Wilson also discusses both the positive and negative aspects of her novels, which analyze "the human capacity to turn love into power-games." He considers them "better than anything written in England in [his] lifetime"; places them in the European tradition of Beckett, Raymond Queneau, Sartre and Canetti; and speaking of her ability to dramatize ideas, to "incorporate metaphysical speculation into the true stuff of fiction itself," concludes that "when the intellectual map of our own times comes to be sketched out, IM will occupy a position analogous to Tolstoy and Dostoevsky in this regard." Wilson perceptively analyzes the influence of Simone Weil, of Sartre's Existentialism and of Martin Heidegger, about whom he asks but doesn't answer: "If for IM, in *Metaphysics as a Guide to Morals*, Heidegger is 'one of the nastiest,' 'dull,' 'devoid of moral judgement' etc...why did she spend the better part of her last active decade reading him and trying to write about him?"

Jackson's Dilemma provides the answer to Wilson's perplexing question. Benet, Murdoch's fictional counterpart, writes by hand instead of using a typewriter or word-processor, and wonders: "what *does* it all mean and why on earth do I go on with it? Am I not losing my German? Could one forgive Heidegger or be interested in him just because he loved the Greeks?" Toward the end of the novel Benet surveys his chaotic manuscript: "His work on Heidegger lay there neglected, unfinished, the sheets covered with his handwriting, piled in confusion. He thought, as he put the sheets roughly together, this is a sort of nemesis.... Sitting down he scanned half a page. No good, *just no bloody good!* ... What was the use of going on like this? Innumerable others had done it better. His love-hate for Heidegger, and for Wittgenstein, was better kept to himself. He was not a scholar. He had really *done*, nothing."

Wilson notes that Iris was also careless about important details (which her copy-editors failed to correct), used repetitive plots in her late fiction and lapsed into self-parody: "the same merry-go-round of emotional entanglements, the same old repetitious metaphysical speculations, the same mage-figure, as it were Canetti or Professor Fraenkel, dominating an increasingly ageing group of friends."

As Wilson began to work on Iris' life, he fell into the common trap of biographers who deal with a living subject and realized why he could never complete it: "IM wants a tame friend to write the book...in order to prevent anyone else doing so. In fact she would want to call

DOI: 10.1057/9781137347909

all the shots and censor what went in." He also made some important discoveries she would not want him to reveal. She habitually described herself as having Anglo-Irish parentage, which was "a good deal more chic than the respectable suburbs of poor old Belfast." She claimed that her paternal aunts were long dead and was furious to learn that Wilson had gone to Northern Ireland and interviewed them. He discovered that the love-child's parents were forced into a shotgun wedding when Iris' mother became pregnant. It would be impossible for him to describe her promiscuous sex life, though readers would certainly want to know about it, while she was alive.

Wilson quickly descends from the high ground of philosophy to a commando attack on gentle John. He compares Iris and John to "naughty children left in charge of a house while their parents were away." Calling John a fluttery old lady and excited macaw, Wilson condemns his extreme right-wing political views and "whooping enthusiasm for capital punishment." He quotes Honor Tracy (Iris' close friend) exclaiming, "Iris has made a fool of him all her married life," and John's confession as early as 1981 (when he was fifty-six) that he'd completely given up on sex. This seems to contradict John's humorous account in *Widower's House* of his unwilling sexual adventures as well as Wilson's assertion about John and Audi Villers, whom John married soon after Iris died: "for the last couple of years of IM's life, Audi and [John] would walk about clasping one another like lovers while a bedraggled old IM tagged behind." Wilson concludes with an account of his radical change of attitude and deadly condemnation: "I had always thought of him as dear, sweet, bumbling, smiling [John], who 'didn't mind a bit' when IM received all the plaudits, achieved international fame and acclaim as a writer of genius, took many lovers and had many friends, and then declined into being a demanding, incontinent old wreck. I changed my view and began to wonder whether, inside this uncomplaining little leprechaun, there was a screaming, hate-filled child who minded very much indeed."

Several emotional factors seem to have provoked Wilson's misguided missiles. He'd once put Iris and John on a pedestal, then resented their profound influence on his life and work, and took pleasure in pulling down the gods that failed. They'd encouraged his calling as a High Anglican priest, but Iris' ideas on religion made him realize that he could "never adhere to what she called the Christian mythology." She had a powerful impact on his early novels and he dedicated the first one, *The Sweets of Pimlico*, to the couple. Iris bitterly hated his divorce from an

DOI: 10.1057/9781137347909

older Oxford don and marriage to an elegant architectural historian. Most importantly, Wilson felt obliged to unmask John's image as a lovable leprechaun. He rejects John's claim that the intensely private Iris would have wanted him to portray her degrading decline into Alzheimer's and is appalled by what he calls "the resentments, envy, poisonously strong misogyny and outright hatred of his wife which seemed to me to come from his books."

II

But let John have the last word. He kept a diary while caring for Iris, and his tender *Elegy for Iris* (1998) illuminates her early life, their courtship and marriage, and some obscure aspects of love, fate and illness. Their love story has tragic overtones as he looks back on their life together through the prism of her Alzheimer's disease, diagnosed in 1995. But he vividly describes their intensified intimacy during her last years (she died soon after the book appeared) when he single-handedly cared for her as she lapsed into a sad but still charming second childhood. His labors were rewarded and he finally, totally, captured as his sole possession the sometimes promiscuous and always elusive Iris. John's witty, stylish and charming *Elegy* appeals to readers by suggesting that Alzheimer's can be jolly good fun, and by making senescent love both pleasing and poignant.

John provides vivid descriptions of Iris' teachers and lovers at Oxford. The appealing Eduard Fraenkel was "a venerable, almost gnomelike figure, shuffling up High Street after giving some class or lecture, surveying the world with a disconcertingly bright and youthful eye." John describes but does not name her long-dead and easily identifiable lovers. Arnaldo Momigliano was "a Jewish Italian professor, another wartime refugee, from London University. He loved her deeply, an affection she sweetly and reverently returned. He was a gentle little man, neat and elderly, and they did not go to bed together (I believed that), but sat talking all evening about the ancient world while he kissed her sometimes and held her hand."

The Hampstead tyrant and monster, Elias Canetti, "made love to Iris, possessing her as if he were a god." John "felt torn between involuntary admiration and strong dislike. Dislike won." Canetti's antithesis, Franz Steiner, was "a real poet, with whom Iris had been very much in love.

DOI: 10.1057/9781137347909

She would possibly have married him had he lived, but he had a serious heart ailment and knew that he could not live long.... She grieved for him deeply. He sounded a delightful man, gentle (like all Iris' close friends, as opposed to her 'gods') and humorous." Frank Thompson also seemed destined for an early death. After he'd joined the army, he asked Iris to marry him, "pointing out that he was sure to be killed before the war was over and she would be able to draw a widow's pension." She tearfully refused his kind but mercenary offer, and agreed to go to bed with him before he went overseas.

The profoundly romantic Iris fell in love easily and with many different sorts of men. Some represented wisdom or spiritual authority, others were darkly ambiguous and enigmatic. "She usually gave her favours out of admiration and respect," John observes, "for, so to speak, the godlike rather than the conventionally attractive or sexual attributes in the men who pursued her." When Iris took her masochistic journeys to see Canetti in London and disappeared into her mysterious evil world, the ever-tolerant John thought it would be vulgar and unseemly to be jealous of her lovers. But she reassured him by saying, "just keep tight hold of me and it will be all right"—and it was.

During their "ecstatic egoism of falling in love," John likens the sturdy and purposeful Iris, who'd been compared to a Shetland pony, to a water buffalo and little bull. They developed a childish intimacy—with pet names, giggling and rubbing noses—and their secret expression, "a kind word," came to mean the promise of a sexual encounter. Iris was then about to publish her first novel, *Under the Net* (1954), which was strongly influenced by an important Irish connection: Samuel Beckett's *Murphy* (1938). John notes "the meticulous way she always planned the more outlandish episodes in her fiction, testing them in her mind with careful common sense to make sure they worked."

John contentedly describes their marriage as *solitude à deux*, "the inward self-isolation of a couple from anything outside their marriage." Their love gave him a deeper understanding of great works of literature—*Troilus and Criseyde*, *Othello* and *The Golden Bowl*—which he analyzed in *The Characters of Love* (1960). When John criticized D. H. Lawrence's "half-baked religiosity" about sex, Iris defended Lawrence by stating that "he was such a marvelous writer, it didn't matter what he wrote about, or how."

John shows that painting played an important part in Iris' life and work. She was deeply moved by Titian's *The Flaying of Marsyas* at a Royal Academy exhibition in London and by Piero della Francesca's

DOI: 10.1057/9781137347909

Resurrection when they made the pilgrimage to his birthplace, Borgo Sansepolcro. He also has some perceptive pages on their friendship with the Canadian realist painter Alex Colville. "His art is meticulous in detail," John remarks, "as he takes infinite pains over extreme niceties of composition, and this precision contrasts with the statuesque solidity of his human figures, as massive and mysterious as Piero's and yet wholly absorbed in the commonplace activities of contemporary life."

My conversations with and letters from Iris, and Conradi's biography, correct some surprising errors in John's *Elegy*. He made them through carelessness, poor memory, lack of curiosity or respect for Iris' privacy. She did not have a "happily godless childhood," but was confirmed in the Anglican church. She did not have an "unusually clear" handwriting; it was often quite difficult to read. John did not teach her to drive in 1955; she drove trucks while working for the U.N. in postwar Europe. She slept with Momigliano on their trip to Italy, and would have married Thompson if he hadn't been killed in the war. Her last novel, *Jackson's Dilemma*, did not receive "exceptionally good reviews"; most critics disliked it. Most significantly, John attributes to Iris his own negative attitude about children.

The heart of John's book concerns Iris' struggle with Alzheimer's. Two revealing photos first show them standing outdoors, Iris holding John's arm, with her intellectual powers intact: vivid, attractive, alert and staring straight out at the camera. Later, in her Alzheimer's years, they're seated, as John looks up at the camera, white-haired, open-mouthed and with his arm protectively around her. Aged, wrinkled and disheveled, with half-closed eyes, Iris looks downward, lost forever in a desolate world of her own.

The first signs of her disease were the inability to concentrate, form coherent sentences or even remember where she was or had been. She tells John (as she told me) that ideas for her last novel wouldn't come together: "It's this man Jackson. I can't make out who he is, or what he's doing." She then becomes constantly anxious and agitated, wants to escape from him but also feels the "terror of being alone." John both identifies with her suffering and feels strangely and self-protectively detached from her.

So John is forced to adopt a new way of life. When Iris finally falls asleep at the end of a difficult day, he types in bed beside her. She occupies herself with meaningless tasks, picking up odd bits of rubbish as she wanders vacantly around the house. They'd never owned a television, but

DOI: 10.1057/9781137347909

she's now fascinated and mercifully distracted by children's programs. He cuts and shampoos her hair, but can't figure out which way her underpants are supposed to go and after a struggle lets her wear her trousers to bed. Like a very nice three-year-old, she needs to be fed, changed and bathed. John finally gets the child he never had or wanted.

Inevitably, there are serious problems: intensified squalor and eruptions of anger. As they descend into chaos and withdraw into their solitary life, John, like Iris earlier on, refuses to accept help when he desperately needs it. He establishes, at last, his long-desired goal: absolute control over the helpless Iris. But even the saintly John has his breaking point. He's sometimes overcome by violent irritation and "uncontrolled fits of exasperation, stamping on the floor and throwing the papers and letters on it, waving [his] hands in the air." One day he suddenly goes completely berserk, curses Iris and says how much he hates her. He screams at his beloved, "you're mad. You're dotty. You don't know anything, remember anything, care about anything." He even, when he's completely enraged and she begs him not to hit her, punches her in the arm. All this abuse simply brings out the natural goodness in Iris.

John was severely criticized for revealing the intimate, humiliating and even disgusting details of Iris' life. But he was ruthlessly honest and taught families how to cope with the disease by facing truth and accepting reality. By sharing his experience he showed people that they were not alone, and that it was normal to get exasperated and behave badly. John could honestly say, in his late memoir *Widower's House* (2001), when "sinking into daily depression and flying into rages...I loved Iris more than I had ever done before, and felt closer to her than I had ever felt before." A passage in Virginia Woolf's "A Sketch of the Past" in *Moments of Being* explains the healing power of John's fine memoir: "It is only by putting it into words that I make it whole; this wholeness means that it has lost its power to hurt me; it gives me, perhaps because by doing so I take away the pain, a great delight to put the severed parts together."

DOI: 10.1057/9781137347909

Index

DOI: 10.1057/9781137347909

DOI: 10.1057/9781137347909

DOI: 10.1057/9781137347909

9 781137 352415